Quality in Action

Quality in Action

93 Lessons in Leadership, Participation, and Measurement

Patrick L. Townsend
Joan E. Gebhardt

John Wiley & Sons, Inc.
New York   Chichester   Brisbane   Toronto   Singapore

Library of Congress Cataloging in Publication Data:

Townsend, Patrick L.
    Quality in action : 93 lessons in leadership, participation, and
measurement / Patrick L. Townsend and Joan E. Gebhardt.
        p.   cm.
    Includes index.
    ISBN 0-471-16136-5
    1. Total quality management.   2. Industrial management.
I. Gebhardt, Joan E.   II. Title.
HD62.15.T69   1992
658.5'62—dc20   91-25776

Printed in the United States of America

10   9   8   7   6   5   4   3   2   1

For Brady and Michael

Foreword

*P*at Townsend and Joan Gebhardt have written an important book. And one that's just plain fun to read.

What *more* can be said about quality? Lots, it turns out. The first task of this book is demystification. Quality is—at many companies—becoming everyone's business. But most books written about quality are a pain to read—daunting math, a blizzard of complex charts and graphs, academic language, an obvious sense of authorial self-importance.

Well, you'll find none of that here. You'll find clear English, cartoons, fables, and cases.

But in the end, you'll also find a button-down scheme. The 93 axioms—on leadership, participation, and measurement—add up to a full-blown theory of quality/quality improvement.

My best recommendation is my own reaction. I would dearly love to develop—and then teach—a year-long factory, operations center, or university course based on this book. I think "students" (workers, bosses, MBAs-in-training) would come out with both a feel for the intangibles of quality and a solid tool kit. And I know that as a teacher, I would have a great time along the way. Moreover, with each reading, I also know that I'd learn something new each time I picked up the book.

In short, Lawrence, Curleigh, and Mough may be the next giants of the quality movement. This book is a gem!

TOM PETERS

Preface

*T*his book has a complex goal: to take the mystery out of quality. Companies and individuals too often seek a linear formula for achieving quality based either on a successful case study or a theoretical model. They expend a great deal of energy looking for a series of logical steps where first you do this, and then you do that, and (presto!) you have quality. Anyone who treats quality as a solely rational exercise misses an essential truth. Quality is not only cerebral, it is emotional; it touches both the heart and the head. But how do you talk about this aspect of quality in a corporate setting? How do you move a company—or a person— from intellectual assent to conviction? That is the mystery.

In the lexicon of the mystery story, "How?" is only one of three questions that must be answered, along with "Who done it?" and "Who profits?" When dealing with quality, the question "Who done it?" is really a question of "Who does it?" and the answer is simple: *You* do. Quality cannot be pushed off onto someone else. Bankruptcy courts are filled with organizations whose people—from top to bottom—assumed someone else was going to take care of quality. The answer to "Who profits?" is equally straightforward: *Everyone* profits from quality:

- Employees of corporations that focus on quality have greater control over their own work lives and more satisfying jobs.

- Customers of these corporations receive greater value for their money than they would have if they had chosen a competitor, even a lower-priced competitor.
- Countless polls and case histories indicate that the owners of these corporations receive an excellent return-on-investment for quality-related expenditures.
- Any corporation that earns and retains a reputation for quality products and/or services gains and retains customers, thereby making more money. Dr. W. Edwards Deming extrapolates this to the creation and preservation of jobs.
- The strength of individual corporations contributes to the nation's economic well-being, enabling it to retain control of its national destiny.

Notice that not all the "profit" is in dollars: Employees, customers, corporations, and nations gain in intangible ways as well.

That still leaves the question of "How?" In the mystery format, that question is traditionally one of opportunity and method. Could Ms. X have done the foul deed with the knife? Could Mr. Y have taken the cash from the safe? The competent detective finds the answer through an analysis of all the facts and feelings leading up to the crime. Seemingly contradictory information is weighed and balanced, red herrings are discarded, and truth emerges in its own untidy fashion.

After reading the myths, fables, and realities awaiting you on the following pages, you will recognize both opportunities and methods to improve quality. Better still, you will have honed your awareness of the atmosphere that surrounds the events, the attitudes that accompany the actions. You will be able to spot red herrings at a glance.

This volume actually consists of three mini-books, providing insights into the three main issues every quality process has to face. The choice of format is illuminated in *An Ancient Fable*, which also provides the first lesson in quality: Everyone has a pet theory about what is most important. Everyone is right—and wrong—at the same time. It is *most* important to pay attention to *all* the facets of improving quality.

The sequence is decidedly nonlinear, if not downright screwy in a number of cases, and if you are addicted to logic, you may be somewhat puzzled (if not irritated) to find yourself asking, "Just what does this have to do with quality?" Relax. Read it for fun. Then read it for information. Then share it with someone. As an employee hand this book to your boss, or as a boss hand this book to your employee, and say, "I think this is interesting (or strange or nonsense or crucial). What do you think?" If half the stories "make sense" the first time through, if a quarter more "fall into place" the second time, and someone else "gets the point" the third time, the mystery will be solved.

PATRICK L. TOWNSEND
JOAN E. GEBHARDT

Holden, Massachusetts
February 1992

Acknowledgments

*T*he number of people who would like to have authored a published book is considerably larger than those who have actually managed to do so. We would still be in that first group were it not for the help and support of a whole crowd of friends and associates who listened to our ideas, encouraged our hopes, and enriched our lives. We wish to extend our heartfelt thanks to each of them.

On the home front, our two sons Michael and Brady and our faithful assistant Jonathan (a somewhat bewildered terrier), put up with late meals and late hours. Our parents formed a formidable four-person fan club where we could turn for unquestioning applause or specific critiques, whichever we needed at the time. Our friends and neighbors, Jan and John Mellecker, Brad and Alyson Gay, Byron and Laura Menides, and Joe and Eileen Reinhardt, laughed at our stories and asked (sometimes unanswerable) questions. Paul Manoogian, our favorite observer of life for the past 20 years, contributed stories of his own and lent us his unstinting support and friendship. Linda Barresi deserves special mention as an invaluable sounding board throughout the project; she helped us strike the balance between fact and fancy.

There are several individuals who made our professional lives immeasurably easier. Larry Abramoff and the many men and women of Tatnuck Bookseller and Sons were pivotal in keeping our first book *Commit to Quality* alive. Without that support we doubt that we ever would have had the courage to write a second book. For over a year, we were a part of the Avatar International Inc. family. We will always be grateful to both Mike Everett and the rest of the training crew for a professional association that was both intellectually stimulating and personally rewarding. The Washington Speakers Bureau under Bernie Swain and Harry Rhoads provided Pat with a working laboratory, giving him the opportunity to visit dozens of companies struggling with quality issues. Many thanks to both of them and all of their wonderful team. Thanks also to Kathy Hannigan and Judy Page of Holden Travel who organized hassle-free travel and to Ken Scott of Holy Cross College who made our computers author-friendly.

Our writing efforts have always been encouraged by Ned Hamson, editor of *The Journal for the Association for Quality and Participation.* He offered us numerous chances to work out new ideas and try them on a real audience. Diane Sherlock and Susie Wallerstein gave us a forum through the PBS Adult Learning Service. Ted Nardin spotted the nucleus of an idea which exploded into a book none of us could have envisioned. Our editor and friend at John Wiley & Sons, Steve Ross, showed faith in us, first by accepting the roughly defined book idea, and then by investing his own overwhelming patience and talent in the final product. We have benefited enormously from his collaboration.

Many companies and individuals have contributed to the contents both directly and indirectly. The Paul Revere Insurance Group, led first by Aubrey K. Reid, Jr., and now by Chuck Soule, continues to be an extraordinary example of what it means to be a "quality company." They provided specific ideas and general inspiration. Fred Smith at Federal Express articulated an important leadership principle for us. Mutual of Omaha's cogent memo on measurement was a real find. The Carthage Machine Company, the Peabody Hotel, the Chicago Downtown Marriott, Pecten Chemicals, Fluoroware, Tennant Company, Daka Inc. at Clark University, North Pacific Paper Corporation, Harden Furniture Company, Intermountain Health Care, Auburn Police Department, and the Cherry Point Naval Aviation Depot were all generous with time and materials.

Our phone calls to Dr. Brent James, Ron Zemke, Chip Bell, Roger Dowd, Roland Dumas, John Denver, Tom Curtis, John Goodman, David Levine and George Strauss, Dick Chase, Noel and Tammy Cunningham, Chuck DeLay, Jeff Pym, Joe McConville, Joe Kraskouskas, G. Lynn Shostack, Captain Ron Miller and Andrew Boyd, and Colonel Jerry Gartman and John S.W. Fargher, Jr., yielded a wealth of information and some first-class conversations. Curt Reimann, the Director of the Malcolm Baldrige National Quality Award, deserves thanks just because of the magnificent job he has done in helping to nurture that marvelous creation to life.

This book took two years to write, so it's not surprising that so many people influenced its mixture of fractured fairy tales and business case studies, military leadership examples and whimsical stories, not to mention real-life experiences. We are indebted to the People to People group that we accompanied on tour throughout Russia, Byelorussia, and Belgium. Their wit and insight helped shape the contents of this book. Bo Edvardsson and Evert Gummesson invited us to lecture in Sweden and acted as our hosts. They also allowed us to pick their brains. Generous hospitality, indeed! Eb Scheuing at St. John's University saw that we got invitations to the Quality in Services Conference held in Connecticut jointly sponsored by that university and the Service Research Center in Sweden; it was a wonderful experience and paid untold dividends.

Throughout, Tom Peters has been a very special friend and a source of inspiration and support. We enjoy both his columns and his wacky notes. The other people who were so generous with their time as to write endorsements for this book will also always hold a special place in our hearts.

P.L.T.
J.E.G.

Contents

On Participation

On Measurement

Quality
in Action

An Ancient Fable

*I*n the land of Ancient, the king had just returned from the annual Conference of Kings. It had been the first Conference he had been to in years. In previous years, there was always some emergency that had to be dealt with, forcing him to cancel his reservations at the last minute.

He was very excited. At the Conference, everyone had been talking about how a truly great country had elephants. Even though he didn't really know what an elephant was, he was sure it was just what was needed to snap his country, Ancient, out of its doldrums.

So he summoned his consultants. (Ancient was a poor country and was not able to afford wise men; it had had to settle for consultants during a budget crunch some years before.) "We need elephants in this land of Ancient," he said.

The consultants, Lawrence, Curleigh, and Mough, said that they were sure they could help locate elephants. "We may even have some already," one of them ventured. "But, first, we should go and inspect somebody else's elephants—so that we will recognize them and be able to tell our Ancient citizens how to identify and raise their own," said another.

"One of our neighbor countries has one in a town not far from our border," the king said, getting even more excited by the positive, can-do attitude of the consultants. "Perhaps one of you could go there."

"I'll go," all three of them said.

"Yes, it would be best if you all went," the Ancient king said. And he gave them the name of the town that was home to an elephant.

The three consultants rode there together, but each was plotting to finish learning about the elephant before the other two did and hurry back to the country of Ancient to begin spreading the word.

They arrived, late at night, at the town that had an elephant. Fortunately, there was an inn with three vacancies so the consultants each rented a room. Lawrence had noticed a couple of signs on the way in to town, indicating where the elephant was located. As soon as he thought the other two were asleep, he snuck out of the inn and went to find the elephant.

It was a moonless night, but he was able to make out the words "Elephant House" on a large building. It was even darker inside, but Lawrence began to feel around for the elephant. He bumped against the elephant's side and marveled at the fact that it felt precisely like a wall. He was going to explore further but he heard a noise. Since he now knew what an elephant was, he hurried out the back door and headed back to the inn to get his horse so that he could begin his ride back to Ancient.

The noise had been caused by Curleigh, who entered the dark room and, grasping in the dark, caught hold of the elephant's tail. "An elephant," he said to himself, "is nothing but a large rope." He was going to explore further, but he heard a noise and quickly exited.

Mough's first encounter with the elephant was with a leg. "Ah ha!" he said to himself. "An elephant is shaped like a tree trunk." Not wanting to delay his return to Ancient for even another moment, Mough left.

The three consultants, each of whom now billed himself as an "Elephant Expert," were soon roaming the land of Ancient, giving speeches on elephants, including hints as to how an Ancient citizen might find an elephant on his or her own. Despite everyone's best efforts, no elephants of any description were found.

The king was very happy that the search for elephants was so vigorous and spirited. "A little competition among the consultants is good," he told the Ancient queen. "Keeps them on their toes."

Finally, someone organized the First Annual Symposium on Elephants. Lawrence, Curleigh, and Mough were to lead a panel discussion as the highlight of the symposium.

After each of them had made their opening remarks, describing their very different views of elephants, the audience seemed confused. One man, an immigrant to the land of Ancient with a reputation as a very practical man (it was rumored that his family had moved there some years ago from a neighboring empire after he, then a young boy, had made some remark about a naked emperor on parade), stood and said, "A friend of mine has sent me a picture of an elephant. I don't understand why your descriptions don't seem to match this picture."

With that, he held up a large and accurate picture of an elephant. There was a stunned silence. Lawrence responded first. "I will agree that some elephants may look something like that. Tomorrow I will produce for the first time a picture of a really top-notch elephant." Curleigh and Mough also promised to bring pictures of truly good elephants with them tomorrow.

The next morning, the meeting room was packed and the air hung heavy with anticipation. Lawrence was the first to raise up his picture. It looked very much like a large section of wall with little legs and feet, a small tail, and a small, funny-looking head. Curleigh's drawing showed a long, very sturdy rope, one end of which was attached to what appeared to be a Chihuahua dog with unusually big ears and a long nose. Mough's depiction of an elephant appeared at first to be a small redwood forest, until you noticed that at the top of the four giant trees was a small body.

Lawrence's wall, Curleigh's rope, and Mough's trees were each drawn very well and were, indeed, very impressive. The moderator quickly pointed out that all of the pictures did appear to include roughly the same components, albeit in different proportions.

The moderator's comments fell on deaf ears. The symposium

broke up shortly after that, amid a good deal of shouting and screaming. It seems that those people who had already paid for the services of any one of the three consultants were not happy with the idea of changing their ideas about elephants. Pledges of loyalty were heard ringing through the hallways. Each of the consultants declared that, next year, they would organize their own symposium.

The Ancient king was not happy, for he knew instinctively that his kingdom now could not be a truly great kingdom. He missed the Conference of Kings the next year. An emergency came up the day before he was supposed to leave.

The moral of this story cannot be understood without a basic understanding of the language of Ancient. "Elephant" in Ancient connotes "Quality Process." The Ancient word for "wall" looks remarkably like the English word for "Leadership," while the words for "rope" and "tree" are much like the English words for "Participation" and "Measurement."

Each of the three main parts of this book—*On Leadership, On Participation*, and *On Measurement*—addresses one of the essential components of a successful, long-lived quality process. Presenting them as separate entities is not meant to imply that they can, or should be, implemented independently of each other. Each needs to be mastered; all need to be balanced as interdependent elements of a cohesive quality effort.

Physically, the three parts of this book are analogous to three jigsaw puzzles, each with 31 pieces illuminating attitudes and ideas, materials and skills. Any piece can be the beginning, and there are hundreds of possible sequences and schemes for assembling the whole. Recognizing that each reader will bring his or her own background to the reading of these ideas, there is no one set way prescribed to go about assimilating the material. Instead, every article has a keyword chosen to stimulate thought and discussion, clue the reader into the content, and serve as an easy indexing tool. These words are arranged in alphabetical order within each part of the book. The axioms at the end of each article are the authors' observations on what does (or does not) contribute to an environment in which quality can flourish.

Taken as a whole, this book provides a foundation for building a unique quality process in any organization ... as long as the individuals involved are willing to make the effort.

Part One
On Leadership

1 Action

Commitment: Taking an Active Role

It is not enough that top management commits itself for life
to quality and productivity. They must know what it is that
they are committed to—that is, what they must do. These
obligations cannot be delegated. Support is not enough;
action is required.   —*Dr. W. Edwards Deming*

They watch your feet, not your lips.   —*Dr. Tom Peters*

Axiom #**1** *Leadership for quality must be active, obvious, and
informed.*

2 Authority

Freedom to Act Encourages Leadership

Acts of leadership can be found at every level of an organization.
That is the belief at Federal Express, winner of the Malcolm
Baldrige National Quality Award in 1990. In a presentation to the
National Quality Forum VI in New York on October 2, 1990,
former Marine Fred Smith, in his dual role as the 1990 chairman
of National Quality Month and as founder, chairman, and CEO of
Federal Express Corporation, took the occasion of a general ses-
sion presentation to talk not only about his company (as many of
his fellow presenters did) but about his people:[1]

I can tell you from my experiences what truly "makes my
day" . . . letters from our customers reminding me who is *really*

responsible for our company's high standards of quality. Take this one from the CEO of Hitachi Data Systems, for example:

> *"The building rumbled and shook to the tremblors* [sic] *of the October, 1989, San Francisco earthquake, but Federal Express courier Maurice Jane't continued to scan each package he was picking up at our company. He struggled to get them down nine flights of stairs through rubble to his waiting van and on to the airport just in time for the plane. An extraordinary example of personal commitment," wrote CEO, Gary Moore.*

Customer Jim Saunders, writing from Columbia, Missouri, described his daily exchanges with FedEx courier Mary Knoll. "Monday through Friday, it's the same routine," Jim wrote. "She's concerned about the way my day is going. I know a number of people she visits every day, so I'm aware of how we all enjoy her. To us, she is not just Mary Knoll—she IS Federal Express."

. . . For us, responsibility and decision-making must be pushed to the person closest to the job. As demonstrated by courier Stephanie Flores, leadership can surface in any corner . . . even in the most unlikely places . . . the middle of a flood in southern Louisiana, for example:

> *Having been informed that the Post Office would not deliver until the waters receded, a Federal Express customer awaiting a payroll shipment assumed we would be experiencing similar problems. Resigned to the fact that she would miss her payroll deadline, she was amazed to see Stephanie wading in water up to her knees toward the front door.*

Smith's conclusion: "As Stephanie and Maurice Jane't and Mary Knoll and employees from every division illustrate, leaders emerge when one is empowered to act."

These leaders do not emerge spontaneously. Smith is obsessed with what he calls the "Human Side of Quality," the theme of National Quality Forum VI. He refers to it as "the common sense side . . . and the foundation for any success we may have had with the quality improvement process. Respect for the dignity of our people demands that we answer some simple and universal questions:

- What do you expect of me?
- What's in it for me?
- Where do I go with a problem?

Employees are backed with tools, training, programs, and processes that enable them to give their best. Employees know what their responsibilities are, and they are granted authority to act as necessary to meet those responsibilities.

Smith notes, "We expect a lot—highly motivated people consciously choosing to do whatever is in their power to assure every customer is satisfied . . . and more. Every day. Without this concentrated effort, attempting a flawless service is really quite futile."

Axiom #2 *When every employee is involved in improving quality, leaders emerge at every level. It becomes unnecessary to micromanage. The only preconditions are that employees know what is expected from them, know that the organization cares for them, possess the resources to do their jobs, and know they have authority to act.*

3 *Challenge*

Assessing Frederick Taylor's Impact on the American Worker

Any change the workers make to the plan is fatal to success.
—*Frederick Taylor [1856–1915]*

Konosuke Matsushita is the founder of and executive advisor for Matsushita Electric Industrial Company. Matsushita is not unfamiliar with American business. Until 1991, his company ran the concession stands at Yellowstone National Park. It also owns

Panasonic, Universal Studios, and a host of other organizations. Speaking to an American audience in the late 1980s, Matsushita delivered a scathing speech on American business:

> We will win and you will lose. You cannot do anything about it because your failure is an internal disease. Your companies are based on Taylor's principles. Worse, your heads are Taylorized too. You firmly believe that sound management means executives on one side and workers on the other, on one side men who think and on the other side men who can only work. For you, management is the art of smoothly transferring the executives' ideas to the workers' hands.
>
> We have passed the Taylor stage. We are aware that business has become terribly complex. Survival is very uncertain in an environment filled with risk, the unexpected, and competition. Therefore, a company must have the commitment of the minds of all of its employees to survive. For us, management is the entire work force's intellectual commitment at the service of the company . . . without self-imposed functional or class barriers.
>
> We have measured—better than you—the new technological and economic challenges. We know that the intelligence of a few technocrats—even very bright ones—has become totally inadequate to face these challenges. Only the intellects of all employees can permit a company to live with the ups and downs and the requirements of its new environment. Yes, we will win and you will lose. For you are not able to rid your minds of the obsolete Taylorisms that we never had.

On February 23, 1990, Dr. Joseph M. Juran, pioneer in the field of quality improvement, gave the summary address at "The Quest for Excellence," an executive conference featuring the 1989 winners of the Malcolm Baldrige National Quality Award. A portion of his remarks included the following reference to the "Taylor system":

> A further observation on lessons learned relates to the use of human resources. Most of our companies still retain a considerable residue of the Taylor system of separating planning from execution. That system evolved about a century ago. Its major premise was that the supervisors and workers of that era lacked the education needed

to plan how work should be done. Hence the planning was turned over to engineers. The supervisors and workers were left with the responsibility of carrying out the plans.

During our century education levels have increased sharply, and have thereby destroyed the major premise of the Taylor system. We are mostly agreed that the system has become obsolete, and that it should be replaced by something else. However, despite much recent experimenting we are still not agreed on what should be that something else. Meanwhile we are failing to make use of our biggest underemployed asset—the education, experience and creativity of the work force.

The reports we have heard at this conference included reference to use of self-managing teams. If I may be permitted another look into my fallible crystal ball, I suggest that self-managing worker teams will become the dominant successor to the Taylor system.

Axiom #3 *Management wisdom changes over the ages. Keeping abreast of current trends—including the trend toward quality improvement through a new relationship between management and nonmanagement—is one component of leadership. Management must face the challenge or concede the field.*

4 *Clarity*
When Is New New?

*T*he age-old problem of distinguishing what is worthwhile from what is merely novel was ably tackled by John Hamilton Moore in the preface to his book on navigation in 1798. The script and the spelling may look strange (most of his "s's" look like "f's"— as in some of Thomas Jefferson's best writings), but his conclusion is still sound:

I am well aware that there are perfons, who, to fhew their own fuperior abilities in an obfure Club, will quibble and carp at fome parts, and fay, that they fee nothing new, &c. To fuch Critics it may be anfwered, that a Triangle was a Triangle before the days of Euclid, and fo it is now; but, if the arranging, digefting, fimplifying, and rendering Navigation attainable to the moft common capacity with all the ufeful Tables contained in one Book, which was never done before, it certainly may be called New, or at leaft an Improvement. How far I have fucceeded is left to the judicious Marine to determine.

Moore's Navigation
Preface to the Thirteenth Edition, enlarged,
by John Hamilton Moore
Teacher of Navigation, Hydrographer and Chart-seller to his
Royal Highness the Duke of Clarence
Stationer's Hall, London
1798
Price Eight Shillings Bound

Axiom *#4 If after your reading and discussions on quality you are able to articulate your thinking more clearly, even in the absence of innovation, it may be thought of as new—or at least an improvement.*

5 *Completeness*
Adding All the Ingredients to the Recipe for Quality

Quality improvement requires a change in corporate culture. That is the conclusion of Roland A. Dumas in an article for *Quality Progress.*[2] He compares most companies' attempts to adopt the program of a "guru" to a surreal cooking lesson:

> Find an expert and ask what ingredient is key to a good cake. Get that ingredient and bake it. Throw it out. Find another expert and ask what ingredient he believes is most critical. Get that ingredient and bake it. Throw out the mess. Repeat. Repeat.
>
> After several years of investigating organizationwide quality programs, my colleagues and I have created that analogy to most programs. If a company were to bake a cake in the same way that it introduces a quality system, that's how the recipe would read.
>
> Managers would process a series of perfectly good ingredients in a seemingly logical manner and serially discard them, occasionally polluting the tools and the environment. This serial cake baking method parallels what happens in the typical companywide program when a company adopts the program of a "guru," including the bias toward a single tool. When the program does not achieve the desired outcome, it is replaced by that of another guru, and so forth. In the end, there is a lot of experience, a lot of costs, and frustration with the elusiveness of total quality.

While he grants that this might have some value as a learning experience, companies that understand from the first that quality is a leadership issue have the advantage. One study tracked training and development expenditures that were made in total quality efforts compared to the problems that typical companies experienced:

> ... We found that about 80% of expenditures went for technical training and installing new systems. Less than 20% was related to management leadership and involvement in the programs.
>
> When respondents were asked where the major problems were, the ratio reversed. Eighty percent of the problems were associated with management leadership, support, and involvement, and 20% related to technical skills. In other words, the Pareto principle was stood on its head: 80% of the effort was going to fix 20% of the problems.
>
> The real issue that quality practitioners voiced was that managers bought systems to install in the organization, but did not really understand the underlying philosophy, much less support the quality programs that they had initiated. The most common experience was that the top levels of the company delegated responsibilities too quickly and continued to demand actions that were incompatible with the new quality standards. In interviews, senior managers showed belief that they had bought technical and management systems that would be strategic additions or changes to their businesses. They were generally not aware that the success of total quality systems required a change in their attitude and behavior.

Companies can learn from the experiences of others. Dumas offers seven key recommendations to avoid common pitfalls:

> Some issues are common enough that we can make some general recommendations in the area of developing and implementing an organizationwide quality effort. These points are by no means substitutes for the guidelines of Deming, Juran, or other experts. Rather, they are empirically derived recommendations that might reinforce or supplement the companywide guidelines. They are the points that, though they might be stated in formal programs, often aren't understood by many companies.
>
> **1.** Quality is a management leadership issue. How management thinks, behaves, and structures systems is the pivotal issue.
> **2.** Take care of the basics. Introducing new systems and technologies when people don't have the fundamental skills to work in the new systems is a prescription for disaster.

3. Implement systems and technical change with social change. People are more receptive to new ways of management and working together when the systems are changing. Implementing social and technical change is synergistic.
4. Focus on some basic concepts. The definition of quality should relate easily to everyone's job. It should be simple and practical.
5. Join the post-charismatic generation. Don't allow famous experts to make all your decisions. None of them has a complete answer, but at the same time, they all have something worthwhile to say. Learn from them all, and then become your own guide.
6. Broaden your scope. Learn from organizations in a variety of industries, even those that are not doing as well as you believe you are.

   Broaden the scope of your effort to include quality of management decisions, the sales process, hiring and promotion, training, and every other aspect of the business. They all influence customer satisfaction.
7. Concentrate on a value-driven approach. Above all, quality is an ethic, a value more important than financial return. When it's held as a higher standard, there is more buy-in from employees. The financial return will reflect the higher customer satisfaction and market acceptance than will a cost reduction approach.

Dumas makes a good point: "No organizationwide system should be adopted until management understands its role in leading by example and creating a quality ethic that is supported by its own systems and daily behavior."

Axiom #**5** *Partial understanding of and involvement in quality can produce only partial success or total failure. Complete success requires a complete process. The only chance for a quality process to truly succeed is for a company to simultaneously attack all the issues: leadership, participation, and measurement.*

6 *Confusion*

TQM = Total Quality Mayhem
When Executives and Employees
Are Out of Sync

> The project I'm on at [a large defense contractor] is sending
> most of its people to one- or two-day TQM classes for Total
> Quality Management. The project manager assigned people
> to dates, routed the list for comments, made changes, and
> then routed the final list for comments before turning it in.
>
> So soon everyone will be doing a quality job and
> satisfying their internal and external customers—or, rather,
> they would have been, had not the list been completely lost
> in the routing. *—Paul, an observer of life*

Quality in the abstract is fairly straightforward. Implementation, however, can lead to confusion and disagreement at even the most basic level. Some of this is serious; some is not. Lost memos are trivial compared, for example, to the wide gulf existing between executives' assessments and employees' assessments of how well things are going in general.

When asked "Have you created a corporate culture that makes quality service a priority?," 90 percent of the 500 executives of service organizations responding to a 1990 Harris poll for John Hancock Financial Services replied that they had. When employees were asked if they were satisfied with their "company's effort to improve quality," only 29 percent characterized themselves as "Very satisfied," with an additional 44 percent admitting to being "Fairly satisfied," according to the American Society for Quality Control (ASQC) survey of 1237 employees conducted by the Gallup organization that same year.

Service executives, at least, were sure that their companies emphasized quality and that employees were aware of that fact.

When Harris asked the question, "How important is quality service to the ultimate success of your company?," 98 percent of these executives rated it as "Very Important." Ninety-two percent of them also said that they had given employees explicit authority to handle customer problems.

Somehow that explicit authority is not enough. The ASQC poll disclosed that only 66 percent of the employees said that they had *ever* been asked to be involved in making decisions about significant aspects of their job—almost a third fewer. This is despite systematic attempts to involve employees in improving quality. When employees were asked if there were any quality improvement processes of any sort in place in their companies, 79 percent said "Yes" (the percentage was 92 percent for foreign-owned companies), with "Suggestion Systems" being the most prevalent approach. Asked if they actually participated in any of the various activities, only 63 percent of the employees said that they did. These results fall far short of total involvement.

It may be fair to conclude that while executives are willing to enlist employees in improving quality, executives and employees are simply not seeing the opportunities in the same way. Part of it may have to do with philosophy. Management too often is ready to settle for passive systems (e.g., suggestion systems) where employees can contribute if they wish. Alternatively, management is content if everybody is impacted by decisions made in the name of quality. Either approach is only marginally effective. Employees are more likely to contribute and to recognize that they have the opportunity to do so when the structure is proactive (e.g., teams), enabling employees to implement decisions themselves. Employees seem to be more aware of the potential of teams than are executives.

Consider the results of these two polls. In 1989, an ASQC/Gallup poll surveyed executives and asked them to rate various possible methods for improving quality. They presented the same list to the employees during the 1990 survey. Some of the comparative answers (i.e., percent rating the item as very important) were revealing:

	1989 *Execs*	*1990* *Employees*
Employee motivation	53%	64%
Actively involved corporate leader	61%	52%
Quality improvement teams	28%	43%
More control over suppliers	18%	36%
Improved administrative support group output	16%	34%

Whether discrepancies raise questions about the level of understanding by many American business executives about what is going on inside their organizations or whether they suggest a genuine lack of agreement on implementing meaningful quality processes is hard to assess.

Even the professionals appear confused about the nuances and subtleties of quality tools available. In a 1987 ASQC/Gallup survey of executives, the following question was included: "How often does your company use the following programs or methods?" One of the nine options offered (respondents could mark more than one response) was "total quality control," a phrase that would appear to be self-explanatory. Total means total—or does it?

Thirty-eight percent of the 615 executives (vice-presidents and above, from big companies and small, service and manufacturing) said that they used total quality control "Very Often." Another 30 percent said that they used it "Often." Sixteen percent said that they practiced total quality control "Sometimes," and six percent responded "Rarely." A mere 4 percent admitted to never employing total quality control in their organizations and, finally, 6 percent of these senior managers claimed not to know whether or not their organization ever used total quality control.

To be fair, executives were not even given a choice such as "Always" to counterbalance the "Never." And the survey failed to indicate how respondents would be able to do something "total" on a rare, sometimes, often, or very often basis. This is a "yes" or "no" choice, total or not total. Right? Assume that the first question had been, "Which of these methods do you use to hold your marriage together?" with "total faithfulness" as an option. Would "Sometimes" be an acceptable response?

Executives have the best opportunity for bringing order to an otherwise confused scenario. Until they are clear about what they expect from quality and how employees can contribute, mayhem will be the order of the day.

Axiom #**6** *Until consensus is reached between executives and employees about how to go about achieving quality, there will be a great deal of wasted effort—or no effort at all.*

7 *Consistency*
Colliding Values Create a Consumer Jekyll and Corporate Hyde

*I*t had been another long day at the office, beginning with that presentation by the head of the warranty service department on why her budget had to be increased to cover additional staff. She had the numbers to prove her case.

"Who are these people who are complaining all the time and sending back all this stuff?" he had asked. "We're working hard, the stuff we sell is better than what our competitor is trying to peddle—especially at the price."

Then there had been the phone call from that guy who got past his secretary by just plain lying about who he was and why he was calling. Claimed he was some big-time investor, but he just wanted to complain. Said he had to talk to the president because he wanted to make sure that *this* time something got done. Such language!

And then the news from the bank. Interest rates were going to be higher than they had planned on. Some convoluted bank-talk about "degree of risk."

The afternoon meeting with his staff had been even worse. His suggestion that they apply for the Malcolm Baldrige National Quality Award had hardly been greeted with cheers. The staff wanted to put off submitting the application; they didn't see how they could do it until they spent a couple of years working through the application and getting all kinds of new programs in place. No one would even guess how much it would cost or how long it would take; they wanted to research it. It just did not make any sense. It seemed like he remembered reading that one of the winners in 1988 just went home one weekend and filled out the application, mailed it in, and won. Simple as that. Maybe he would go ahead and give it a try anyway.

The article about the company in the afternoon paper had not helped a bit. *That* had not been solely their fault.

"Oh, well," he thought, "another day, another dollar—or whatever a dollar is worth nowadays. Time to head home. It'll all still be here tomorrow."

On the way home, his car hesitated at the first light. The light was green, his foot was pressing on the gas pedal, but the car thought about it for a second or two before going forward—the same problem he had before he had sent it in for service! He would fill that service manager's ear in the morning.

He decided to stop and buy a fancy dessert to take home. After a day like today, he deserved it. And his family would enjoy it. After looking at the options available in the "Frozen Goodies" section of the supermarket, he narrowed the choice to two, and picked the more expensive one. It was a safer bet, he decided, since neither brand was familiar.

When he got home, his wife told him that the laundry had not had his shirts ready by 4:00 as promised . . . someone would have to go back to the store before 7:00 to pick them up. "I'll go," he said. "I want to talk to them about their poor service. I'm really tired of it."

At least there was something on the evening schedule he enjoyed. The next day was his young daughter's birthday, and once she had gone to bed, he would assemble her new bike. He really liked to putter around like that; it was a great change of pace, and he had always been good with his hands.

When he opened the box, the first thing he did was check to make sure all the small parts and screws were included. To his surprise, they were. About a half-hour later, however, he found out that the seat did not, would not, could not fit into its place no matter how hard he pushed. It only took a couple of minutes of inspection to find the large "burr" an inch or two inside the pipe that the seat was supposed to fit down into.

"Doesn't anyone care about quality anymore?" he asked his wife over dessert. The pie he had chosen was mushy. "How can people stand to produce such junk?"

Axiom **#7** *Americans are becoming more sensitive to quality in their role as consumers. Dr. Armand Feigenbaum has determined that in 1979 quality was given priority equal to price in only 30–40 percent of all buying decisions by consumers. By 1988, that figure had risen to 80–90 percent. To be consistent, Americans must also become more sensitive to quality in their role as business people. They can no longer resent being held accountable for the quality of their own goods and services.*

8 Doctrine
Insight from a Second Reading of Doctors Deming and Peters

*I*n a discipline where doctrine is too often divided into proponents of quality as either science or art, Dr. W. Edwards Deming and Dr. Thomas (Tom) Peters each possess the reputation that could logically be associated with the other.

Dr. Deming, the dean of the worldwide quality movement, is known to most as a "statistics freak." It is true that Dr. Deming's educational background and degrees are in statistics, and that he expects measurement to be an integral part of any quality effort.

If his Fourteen Points are reviewed, however, there is not a number in there anywhere. His book *Out of the Crisis* is much more a discussion of management philosophy than it is a call to use numbers wherever possible.

Tom Peters, the widely popular speaker, author, and management theorist, M.B.A. and Ph.D. in Business, is, on the other hand, widely considered a "humanist," someone with a soft approach to quality improvement. Perhaps because he mixes humor and a dash of the outrageous into his presentations, Peters is associated more with the warm, fuzzy side of management theory than with hard numbers.

His *Thriving on Chaos*, however, repeatedly calls for measurement, for hard data on which to base decisions. Considering that he also has a B.S. and M.S. in Civil Engineering, this is probably not surprising.

Both men are, of course, correct. Only through an approach that combines accumulating necessary data and treating employees with dignity can long-term quality be achieved.

Axiom #8 *Familiarity with the writings of the quality gurus can furnish unexpected insights. Nuances are not always obvious on the first reading.*

9 *Flexibility*
Using Leadership Styles

*L*eaders have a choice of three distinct styles of leadership: authoritarian, participative, and delegative. How effective you are as a leader depends on how well you understand these three options and how flexible you are in applying them. No one person should practice one style all the time, nor can one style be completely avoided by a successful leader. Choosing which style to use in which situation makes leadership both difficult and satisfying.

Authoritarian leadership has gotten a bum rap. Although subordinates may find it objectionable, there are occasions when it is appropriate:

- The leader is making a decision in a situation where time is of the essence.
- The leader has all the necessary information.
- The subordinates have high morale.

These occasions are extremely rare, but many bosses choose this style even when it is inappropriate because of its apparent simplicity; there are no explanations to give or discussions to engage in—the leader just orders his or her subordinates to accomplish the desired task.

Authoritarian leadership is ineffective if used over a long period of time. Morale in an organization can only remain high when the predominate leadership styles are participative and delegative. Only then will employees respond to an authoritarian approach, realizing that its practice signals an unusual situation and knowing that explanations will come when time permits.

Participative leadership is more complex than authoritarian leadership. When time and circumstance allow, the leader includes her or his subordinates in a discussion of the situation and the options. By seeking their opinions and helping them to understand the ramifications of the decision, the leader not only benefits from their knowledge but also obtains the subordinates' support of the decided action—and he or she makes it possible for subordinates to adjust quickly if events do not unfold as expected.

By practicing participative leadership, a leader retains both authority and responsibility for the final decision; he or she makes the call—and gets the blame if things go wrong. After considering and discussing the various options offered by subordinates, the participative leader announces the decision and the reasoning behind it.

The toughest type of leadership to practice is delegative leadership. While the leader continues to have the responsibility for the final outcome of whatever decisions are made, the authority for making that decision is delegated to a subordinate, perhaps with a message along the lines of, "I'm on the hook for this one, but I want you to be in charge of getting it done." Placing the success of one's career into someone else's hands is the strongest proof of trust and respect one person can give to another.

The payoff for effective delegative leadership is enormous. If a leader builds a group of subordinates to whom he or she can confidently delegate authority, the capabilities of the organization are expanded significantly.

Axiom #9 *Leadership techniques can be learned. While there is no question that some people are born natural leaders, the existence of great leaders is no excuse for the rest of us not to endeavor to become competent leaders ourselves. No one uses Einstein's genius in math as an excuse for not being able to balance the checkbook. Quality begins with leadership, and learning leadership begins with an appreciation of the options available.*

10 *Focus*

Policies and Principles

POLICY STATEMENT

Carthage Machine Company is committed to continuously improving
our ability to anticipate and satisfy our customers' needs.

• • •

Better satisfying our customers' needs requires that
the company and its employees are dedicated to a policy of
continuous improvement in all functions and operations.

• • •

All departments will have specific goals that are consistent
with this commitment and those goals will be continuously measured.

• • •

Our progress toward achieving continuous improvement will
bring the quality of Carthage products and services
to a world-class level.

Robert A. Skodzinsky
President

Mark D. Robinson
Chief Engineer

David G. Sabel
Treasurer/Director of Operations

Katie Pais
Controller

Darrel Vertanen
Sales Manager

Milton E. Howard
Plant Manager/New York

Gary Holmes
Plant Manager/Mississippi

Frederick C. Buduson
Quality Process Coordinator

CARTHAGE
MACHINE COMPANY

PRINCIPLES

General management will provide leadership and be actively
involved in the continuous improvement process.

* * *

We believe that quality and productivity gains will be
realized through process control and process improvements.

* * *

We will use process control methods in our
manufacturing operation.

* * *

Annual improvement goals will be developed for each department
by its members.

* * *

We will focus on the prevention rather than the detection
of problems.

* * *

All employees will have opportunities for developing current
skills and learning new ones.

* * *

We will continuously strengthen long term relationships with
customers and suppliers by achieving mutually beneficial
goals.

Axiom #**10** *Policy statements and principles should be brief, clear, and believable. They are used as a touchstone for all employees to gauge whether or not actions are in conformance with the standards and values of the company's quality process. Milliken & Company, a 1989 recipient of the Malcolm Baldrige National Quality Award, focuses its employees on its quality policy by printing it on the back of all its business cards.*

11 Growth
Eleven Leadership Principles to Emulate

*M*ilitary leadership principles have been forged over 25 centuries in situations where the penalty for error can be severe and immediate. Beginning in the sixth century B.C. with the Chinese strategist Sun Tzu, these principles have been refined and developed until today they are used to teach 18-year-olds leadership basics. They can also provide a rich source of personal growth and development guidelines for business leaders.

The United States Marine Corps prescribes 11 principles in the *Guidebook for Marines*, which is issued to officers and enlisted men; each service has a similar list. In slightly condensed (and somewhat translated) form, these principles are universal:

- **Take responsibility.** If you wish to lead, you must be willing to assume responsibility for your actions as well as those of the people who report to you. Use your authority with judgment, tact, and initiative.
- **Know yourself.** Be honest when you evaluate yourself. Constantly seek self-improvement. If you believe that you are truly the best in your department, admit that to yourself. Then set out to be the best in your entire organization.

- **Set an example for others to follow.** Your subordinates look to you for a standard of correct behavior. The manner in which you conduct yourself is more influential than any instructions you may give or any discipline you may impose.
- **Develop your subordinates.** Tell your people what you want done and when you want it completed. If you are confident of your own abilities, then you will also believe in the competency of your subordinates. Answer requests for advice, but leave the details to them.
- **Be available.** Be sure that employees clearly understand their tasks. Tell them why they are being asked to carry out certain duties. Stay aware of their progress and the problems they are encountering, but do not take any initiative away from them.
- **Look after the welfare of your employees.** Know their problems, and make sure that they receive all appropriate help and benefits that they need, but do not pry. Respect their need for privacy.
- **Keep everyone well informed.** Take action to stop rumors; rumors only cause undue disappointment and unwarranted anger. Make sure that people know that they can always look to you for the truth. Then when there is something you can not tell them, they will understand.
- **Set goals that are achievable.** Setting unrealistic goals creates frustration and hurts morale. If you set reasonable objectives, successes will be more easily reached.
- **Make sound and timely decisions.** If you think that you have made a bad decision, have the courage to change it—before it is too late.
- **Know your job.** Stay abreast of current events in your field. Talk with people who have recently attended seminars or those who have shown expertise in areas that you are unfamiliar with. Do not look back to the way things were done in "the good old days."
- **Build teamwork.** Whenever possible, assign projects to your entire staff. Train employees so that they understand

the contributions that each one makes to the entire effort. Insist that everyone pull his or her share of the load. When something goes well, celebrate it.

Axiom #**11** *Although the applications may vary in the military and business worlds, principles of military leadership are based on fundamental truths that make them appropriate in any situation in which one person is trying to lead another.*

12 **Housekeeping**
A Quality Process Starts at Home

*T*he top management of a company has two major sets of customers to worry about. One is the group of people and organizations who pay money for the company's services and/or products. The other is the employees. Without the cooperation of the latter group, the loyalty of the former is always in jeopardy.

To simply exhort employees to provide worry-free products and services without providing a worry-free work environment is folly. One of the major responsibilities of top management is to take care of the housekeeping details that create and maintain an environment in which it is not only possible but probable that continuous improvement can become a norm.

Employees have myriad concerns from safety to flexible scheduling, from benefits to child care. Finding out what is needed to establish a set of conditions conducive to peace of mind is accomplished in the same way as finding out what external customers want—ask.

A good option is an "attitude survey," a survey administered to all employees that focuses solely on opinions about the organization itself rather than on services or products. Such surveys can either be purchased (perhaps from a central industry association) or homegrown. The advantage of buying a standardized survey is that normative data will be available, enabling the organization to compare its relationship with its employees to that found in other companies. If a standardized survey is used, some questions specific to the organization can be added.

As with any survey, what is most important is how the results are used. Publishing results promptly is only the first step; standards for response must be clearly defined. One approach is to announce that any question that elicits 30 percent or more negative responses or is more than 10 percentage points "worse" than the industry norm will be specifically addressed.

Statements of intent are not sufficient; concrete action must follow. Since employees were asked to identify the existence of the problems, it is only fitting that the employees be involved in determining possible solutions. Employees at every level from every department can contribute to the effort. What the organization gains is the opportunity to bring a fresh set of ideas and thinking to what are most likely long-standing concerns.

Paul Revere Insurance Group used this approach at the outset of their Quality Has Value process. An employee attitude survey was purchased from an insurance industry group, expanded to include some questions specific to Paul Revere, and administered to all employees.

The "negative" responses were divided into six logical groups: Supervision, Job Duties, and Training; Work Group Climate/Communications; Salary and Benefits; Chance for Advancement/Job Security; Physical Setting; and Work Schedules. Volunteers were called for.

Each topic was given to a cross-functional, cross-level Action Team. The teams were given full cooperation from the appropriate staff member(s) and the opportunity to make their recommendations directly to the top management. A special Action Team Report for each topic was sent to all employees, complete with recommendations.

Teams were not promised that what they recommended

would be implemented; they were promised an attentive audience who knew that the company was watching. Top management responded to every point. A response of "No" was a valid option as long as it was accompanied by a sensible explanation.

The Work Schedules Action Team led by Sharon Gaudreau, for example, addressed Home Office employee concerns regarding the following four questions:

"How satisfied are you with the hours you work?"
"Do you like the current flex hours options we have?"
"How satisfied are you with your sick leave benefits?"
"How satisfied are you with your vacation benefits?"

Final recommendations were based on:

- Interviewing a cross-section of over 500 employees (management and nonmanagement) throughout the company to get a true understanding of the problems and concerns of all employees in each division.
- Reviewing past company studies and quality ideas within the company.
- Surveying other companies (local, insurance industry, etc.) and comparing policies.
- Studying several documents and material on different types of work schedules.

The recommendations of the Action Team called for significant changes in both the sick-day policy and vacation policy. Both were quickly approved by the company president. In addition, a pilot program for full flex-time was instituted, and another recommendation to change the work week was placed under further study. All the results and their sources were publicized throughout the company.

Top management's willingness to "let the employees in" on the decision-making process was a further demonstration of Paul Revere's commitment to the quality process in general and, in particular, to its belief that its employees are intelligent, well-intentioned adults.

Axiom #**12** *Federal Express Corporation is right. It isn't enough for employees to have the answer to "What do you expect from me?" It is also necessary for employees to know "What's in it for me?" Companies that take care of their employees have employees that take care of their outside customers.*

13 *Humor*
Leave 'Em Laughing

A quality process can provide unique opportunities for humor. Did you ever see a company president wrestling with a boa constrictor or dishing out ice cream? Both events took place in the context of a quality process. While quality is serious business, it does not preclude lightheartedness. Having fun and being serious are not mutually exclusive; Dickensian workplaces were not appropriate even in the time of Dickens.

As with so many things, it is up to the president or CEO to set the tone. At Mutual of Omaha Companies, President Jack Weekly is known as a no-nonsense, bottom-line businessman. Yet he is well liked by the employees—in large part because of his willingness to take chances in front of them.

At the launching of its 100 percent employee involvement quality process in early 1991, the company had Jim Fowler, the host of Mutual of Omaha's long-running *Wild Kingdom* program, help introduce the process. Jim brought some friends from the Omaha zoo. One of them was a 20-plus-foot-long boa constrictor. In an unplanned addition to the program, he invited Weekly up on stage to help handle the snake. Weekly's game grappling with the reptile—including ineffective attempts to stop the snake from invading the inside of his suit coat and trousers— brought whoops of laughter and appreciative applause when

Jim finally released Weekly from his duties as an assistant snake handler.

At the Paul Revere Insurance Group, Aubrey K. Reid was the president of the company from the inception of its 100 percent involvement Quality Has Value process in January 1984 until his retirement seven years later. His ability to have fun, to use humor to express his obvious pride in the accomplishments of employees, was of invaluable benefit to the growth and stability of the process.

One example of his voluntary participation in a delightfully incongruous situation happened in 1988. Shortly after Paul Revere received a visit from the Malcolm Baldrige National Quality Award Examiners (one of two in the service category that first year of the Baldrige), all employees received invitations to have a sundae at "Aubrey's Chestnut Diner" by way of a thank you. (The Paul Revere headquarters is located on Chestnut Street in Worcester, Massachusetts.) On the appointed day, as employees went through the cafeteria line, they were tickled to see Aubrey and his direct reports, decked out in special aprons (bearing the logo of the Chestnut Diner—a picture of Aubrey in a chef's hat), making customized, free ice cream sundaes for everyone.

That same year, Paul Revere's 5th Annual Quality Celebration was kicked off with a "Quality Rap"—a videotape shown on the main stage screen of elegant Mechanics Hall. In it, top managers, bedecked with fedoras and sunglasses, performed a carefully choreographed and thoroughly rehearsed "rap," thanking the employees for their many contributions to the continuously improving quality of the company. It was received with thunderous applause and talked about for months.

Out of context, however, efforts on the part of executives to be "fun people" do not work. The following year, another company that had made several desultory attempts at beginning quality processes, but without an equal degree of top management commitment, decided to duplicate the Paul Revere management team's success. They too made a rap video and showed it at their annual gathering.

Everybody was slightly embarrassed.

Humor only works when it is an accurate reflection of the goodwill within the organization. Showing a sense of humor, taking the chance on looking foolish, takes a knowledge of and sensitivity to what is going on inside the company—and more than a little courage and self-confidence. The top management is, in a very real way, asking for the hearts and minds of its employees when it initiates a 100 percent quality process. It is only fair that the employees should know that the executives' hearts and minds—and senses of humor—are also on the line.

Axiom #**13** **Humor:** *1. The quality of anything that is funny or appeals to the comic sense. 2. The ability to appreciate or express what is amusing, comic, etc. (Funk & Wagnall)*

Good leaders have a sense of humor and know how and when to use it.

14 Identity
This Corporate Identity Is All It Is Quacked Up to Be

*C*ompany values can be communicated in powerful, nonverbal ways with genuine results. The elegant Peabody Hotel in Memphis, Tennessee, owes its unique identity to a prank that became a tradition, a tradition that tells customers, "We care about the little things; we have a splendid past; we have a sense of humor; we are special."

In the late 1930s, Frank Schutt, general manager of The Peabody, and a hunting buddy, Chip Barwick, Sr., returned from a weekend hunting trip in Arkansas. In those days, it was both legal and common practice to use live ducks as decoys, so it occurred to the two (it is generally accepted that some Tennessee sippin' whiskey may have been involved in the decision making) that putting their decoy ducks in the "beautiful but barren Peabody fountain" was a grand idea.

Those first ducks—"three small English call ducks"—established themselves as residents, much to the delight of all. Schutt was smart enough to know a good thing when he saw it; the ducks stayed.

Now the "Duck March" is a twice-daily event at the hotel. The hotel's literature describes the duck parade:

> The tradition begins each morning at 11:00 A.M. with the unrolling of a 50-foot red carpet which stretches from the fountain to the hotel elevators. Peabody duck-keeper, Edward D. Pembroke, who has trained and chaperoned the ducks since 1940, calls for the ducks at their penthouse on the roof. In regal style, the ducks march single file to the waiting elevator and descend to the lobby. The elevator doors open and the ducks, still in single file, waddle across the red carpet, flanked on both sides by uniformed bellboys, to the lobby fountain to the sounds of John Philip Sousa's "Stars and Stripes Forever" or "King Cotton March." With a splash, the mallards take their place in the fountain where they happily spend the day. Each evening at 5:00 P.M., the ceremony reverses and the Peabody ducks—(one drake "lead duck" and four hen mallards)—ceremoniously are returned to their penthouse high atop The Peabody overlooking the Mississippi River.

The Peabody has established for itself an unchallengeable, individual identity among hotels worldwide. It has sent a series of positive signals to its employees and its customers by taking this unique event and doing it extraordinarily well. (And it *is* done extraordinarily well. If the ducks merely ran amuck in the lobby twice a day, it would be quite strange and off-putting.) Customers see this pageant as a public demonstration of the competence and level of care that the entire hotel staff gives to the fine details. Guests, it is implied, will get the red-carpet treatment, too.

Do the ducks have any actual impact on the bottom line? The management of The Peabody believe that they do. For one thing, when people stay at The Peabody, they tell their friends about it. There is no better advertisement than the unsolicited endorsement of a neighbor or friend. Recently a best-selling novel used The Peabody as a setting, calling it "the South's grand hotel." Then again, the lobby fills to overflowing twice a day. Many duck watchers have a drink while they wait or take home a souvenir emblazoned with the picture of a duck—a Peabody Duck, that is.

Axiom #**14** *Like it or not, every company has a corporate identity. It behooves a company to align its external image with its internal values. Often this can be accomplished through the use of symbols: Maytag and its lonely appliance repairman, Disneyland and its cheerful Mickey Mouse, the Peabody Hotel and its daily duck parades.*

15 Internalization
When Instinct and Habit Merge

On February 24, 1989, a cargo door blew off of United Airlines Flight 811 while taking off from Hawaii on its way to New Zealand. Nine people were killed in the explosion, but the plane managed to return to Hawaii with no further loss of life.

In the course of extensive interviews following the incident, the pilot, Captain David M. Cronin, repeatedly credited the fact that both he and his crew had been through "command leadership resource management" training as the major factor in their ability to fly the crippled aircraft safely. At a time when authoritarian leadership would have previously been the norm, Cronin and his crew knew there were other alternatives.

The 35-year United veteran explained that the training stressed the delegation of duties within the cockpit and the importance of having crew members question their captain's actions and offer suggestions. By combining technical experience with leadership training, the crew was able to overcome a situation that was not contained in any "how-to-solve" manuals.

Cronin described how several times during the 24-minute emergency, he took time to discuss things with the other professionals in the cockpit. "In the old days the other crew members didn't speak or do a thing until the captain told them to. Those days are now over," said Cronin.

Early in the emergency, the copilot, Gregory S. Slader, hesitated to follow normal procedure that called for extending the wing flaps to slow the descent of the airplane. He checked first with Cronin, who told him to hold off. Slader agreed.

The flight engineer contributed by using an emergency procedures manual to extrapolate the proper landing speed for a plane with two disabled engines and a flap problem (a situation not covered in the body of the text).

Closer to landing, Cronin accepted Slader's recommendation to extend the wing flaps beyond the point that he, Cronin, thought appropriate—and the copilot proved to be right.

Some of the flight attendants later told investigators that it was one of the smoothest landings they had ever experienced.

Axiom #15 *A time constraint is the most common justification for the use of authoritarian leadership. In an emergency, most leaders instinctively take charge. The appropriate use of authoritarian leadership, however, is rarer than most people think—even when there is a pressing interest in getting things right the first time. Training helps individuals internalize participative and delegative skills. The rest is up to the individual.*

16 *Investment*

Quality: The Best Investment for the 1990s

*T*o be successful in the 1990s, top management needs to have a firm understanding of the relationship between quality and cost. Quality products cost less to produce and, paradoxically, can command higher prices in the marketplace because consumers have been trained to believe that quality costs extra.

The link between high quality and high price has been borne out in two surveys commissioned by the American Society for Quality Control (ASQC) and conducted by the Gallup organization. In the 1988 survey, American consumers were asked how much extra they would pay, if anything, for a quality product.

Specifically, they were asked to assume that they had decided to buy an average product at a particular price and then to decide whether they would pay more for a guarantee that the item would actually meet the expectations that accompanied the initial price. If they would be willing to pay more, they were asked how high they would go.

When the item in question was a $12,000 automobile, 82 percent of those questioned said that they would pay more. In fact, in order to secure a "quality $12,000 automobile," they would pay, on average, $2518 more. Similarly, 94 percent said they would pay $20 above a baseline price of $30 in order to make sure the shoes they purchased measured up to their expectations.

In the ASQC survey the following year, American executives were asked a similar question: "If an American consumer had a choice of two products—one of average quality and one he or she thought was of higher quality but cost more—how much more, if anything, do you think the consumer would be willing to pay to get the higher-quality product?"

For a $12,000 automobile the executives' average response was $2674, and for a $30 pair of shoes the executives estimated that consumers would pay an additional $20. These figures are in line with what consumers say they would be willing to pay.

Consumers and executives agreed: People are willing to spend more in the hopes that the extra money spent will bring them the peace of mind that comes with services and products that are trustworthy.

The other side of the equation yields an interesting question: Is an increase in price warranted to meet the consumer expectations associated with the initial cost? In other words, does it cost the producer more to produce a quality item? The answer is no. Quality products and services are *cheaper* to produce since they do not include the cost of waste or warranty work that have to be recouped when setting a price.

This answer is confirmed by a study of the "Cost of Quality," sometimes referred to as the "Cost of Nonconformance" or the "Cost of Non-Quality." Whatever its name, this concept clearly demonstrates that there is a hidden cost to doing things wrong, a very real cost for every organization—be it in the manufacturing, service, or public sectors.

The components that make up this drain on the budget are prevention, detection, correction, and correction-failure. The last component is the most difficult to measure since it includes business lost because of mistakes. About all that can be said with accuracy about correction-failure losses is that they are most likely underestimated.

In 1989, the same ASQC survey of American executives cited above included this question: "Poor quality as measured by repair, rework and scrap costs, returned goods, warranty costs, inspection costs, and lost sales is said to cost American businesses billions of dollars annually. How much does poor quality cost your company, as a percent of gross sales?"

The responses varied widely and indicate that few executives understand just how costly it is not to produce an item right the first time, on time, every time:

Estimated % of Gross Sales	% of Respondents
Less than 5%	45%
5–10%	18%
10–19%	8%
20–29%	5%
30–49%	3%
50% or more	*
Don't know	21%
Total	100%

less than one-half of one percent

Statistics based on actual measures of a wide sampling of American businesses indicate that the average Cost of Quality is extremely high: 30–35 percent of gross sales for a manufacturing firm and in the mid-30's for a service organization. Either most of the executives surveyed in 1989 worked for superior companies or very few were aware of the true impact of Cost of Quality.

Executives who understand the potential savings and institute a quality process that lowers the cost of producing a service or product have an interesting decision to make. Since costs are now lower, they can lower prices, undercutting their competition while maintaining at least the same profit margin. Or, once they earn a solid reputation for quality (and, of course, lower their internal costs), they can raise prices. Americans, after all, expect to pay more for quality.

Axiom #**16** *Attention to quality can increase a company's profits by lowering production costs, or by making it possible to charge higher prices, or both. There is no better long-term investment.*

17 _Judgment_

Putting Leadership Theory into Practice: Get the Flagpole Up!

_T_hree young lieutenants arrived at their new base together and reported to the adjutant, eager to get going on their first assignment. The base adjutant, a wise old major, had a problem. There were three job openings for young lieutenants, but only one was desirable, just the thing to start a future general on his way. The second job was pretty routine, and the third job was downright dull. Looking at the record books of the three, the major found little difference among them.

To help decide which lieutenant to assign to which job, the major posed them a problem: "I need to get a flagpole raised this afternoon. I am going to give you a list of all the equipment available to you, and I will assign you a sergeant and four troops, all excellent. I want each of you to go away for one hour and then return and tell me how you would go about getting the flagpole up. Your responses will determine the job I assign you."

An hour later, the major called one of the lieutenants into the office and asked, "How would you do it?" The young officer showed the major all of his calculations and explained how he would direct each person in order to get the flagpole up. He said that he was sure they would be able to follow his directions since the major had said that the sergeant was capable and, besides, he, the lieutenant, would be right there with them while the flagpole was going up.

The next lieutenant told the major that she would take the list of equipment and sit down with the sergeant and the four troops, explain the assignment, and ask for suggestions. After listening to them and discussing appropriate points with them, she would make her decision and explain it to them. Then they could get busy. She anticipated having lots of good ideas because the major had spoken so highly of the personnel.

The last lieutenant told the major, "I would turn to the sergeant and say, 'Sergeant, put up the flagpole. If you need me, holler. Otherwise, come get me when you're finished.'"

The major had no trouble making a decision after the interviews.

Axiom #**17** *If you understand the three leadership styles, you won't have any trouble with the textbook answer to this problem: The delegative approach is the most effective use of time and resources. Anyone willing to delegate when possible has time available for other tasks. There are, however, sometimes factors within an organization that make another choice appear desirable. Maybe the habits of the company make participative leadership the norm. Maybe those habits could be changed. There are always choices.*

18 Listening
Hearken! Herein Lies a Story

The Magpie's Nest
An English Folk Tale

Once on a time when pigs spake rhyme, the Thrush, the Owl, and the Blackbird, the Sparrow and the Turtle Dove, all came to call on Madge Magpie. They sat on the branches above her and all began to sing at once:

> "Madge Magpie! Oh, Madge Magpie,
> Pray will you teach us how
> To build such nests as you do
> Upon the swaying bough?

"There's no one in the tree-tops
Who knows so well as you
How birds should build their houses!
Caw, caw! Tu-whit, tu-whoo!"

So Madge Magpie flicked her tail and blinked her eyes and said:

"Come sit in a circle about me,
If you'll listen I'll tell you how
To build just such nests as I do
Way up on the swaying bough."

First she took some mud and made it into a cake.
"Oh, that's how it's done, is it?" cried the Thrush—

"Quit, quit, quit!
That's all there is to it!
I know it all! I know it all!
Quit, quit, quit!"

And off she flew in a hurry. So that's all the Thrush ever learned about how to build a nest. Then Madge Magpie took some twigs and twined them around in the mud.
"Oh, that's how it's done, is it?" cried the Blackbird.

"Muds and twigs! I saw! I saw!
I know it all! Caw, caw! Caw, caw!"

And off she flew in a hurry. So that's all the Blackbird ever learned about how to build a nest. Then Madge Magpie put another layer of mud over the twigs.
"Oh, I knew all that before I came," cried the old Owl.

"Tu-whit, tu-whoo! I knew! I knew!
I'll build my nest as I always do!"

And away he flew in a hurry.
So that's all the Owl ever learned about how to build a nest. Then Madge Magpie lined the nest with feathers and soft stuff to make it snug and cozy.
"Oh, bother!" cried the Sparrow. "I've heard enough!"

"Chip, chip!
Chip! chip!
I know enough!
And now I'll skip!"

And away he flew in a hurry. So that's all the Sparrow ever learned about how to build a nest. Then Madge Magpie looked around and saw that the only bird left was the Turtle Dove. But the Turtle Dove hadn't paid attention any of the time. She had just kept talking and talking herself. Madge had a twig in her mouth to weave around the outside of the nest to make it all firm and strong, when she heard the silly Turtle Dove crying: "Coo! Coo! Take two, Taffy, take two! Take two-o-o-o!" And Madge Magpie said:

"No, you don't take two. Take one! One's enough!"
But the Turtle Dove only said: "Coo! Coo! Take two!"
"One's enough, I tell you," cried Madge, "only one!"
But the Turtle Dove would not listen. She liked only to talk herself! "Coo! Coo! Take two-o-o-o!"

And then Madge Magpie cried: "Alas! How can I teach silly birds to build nests if they will not *listen* to what I say?" And away she flew. Nor would she ever again tell any of them what to do.

Axiom #**18** *This is a children's story, and it is possible to get the message after the first bird flies away. Or is it? The first part of the tale teaches one lesson: If you don't hear all the directions, it is impossible to do the job right. The last paragraph carries another lesson: If you don't listen until the end, you alienate others. Like the magpie, co-workers resent not getting a complete hearing. No matter how simple you think a message is, listen until the end.*

19 Love
Leadership at Its Best

*T*he English language, so rich in variety that there is a network of words for expressing virtually every nuance of any central concept, has been strangely abused in one key area—love. We have come to limit its meaning, on the personal level, to two instances—family and sex. We are uncomfortable, for instance, to hear of a person loving another of the same gender, or of a married person admitting love for a member of the opposite sex other than a spouse.

Yet there are many manifestations and varieties of love, and one of the greatest is good leadership. We acknowledge this with statements such as "he really loves his people" or "they really love her," but we rarely look past these cliches. Love and leadership are not synonymous terms, but leadership is a form of love; and our knowledge and experience of the root concept can provide us with useful insights into leadership.

Perhaps the most obvious thing that leadership and love have in common is the act of caring about the welfare of someone other than oneself—an act that is central to both. One's love for another implies caring about his or her well-being, physical and mental. Conversely, a failure to notice, or to obviously care about, a decline in the quality of someone's state of existence is taken as proof that "You don't love me anymore," and the relationship will deteriorate. This is true even in business. If the "led" perceive that the leader doesn't care about nonbusiness facts that affect employee welfare—for example, that there is no parking available—that person will quickly be judged a poor leader.

Those who would call themselves leaders must be capable of love, of allowing themselves to be loved, and of understanding the awesome responsibilities incurred when one seeks and accepts the love of others. To love someone is to make a commitment to him or her. It is not a pledge to nag someone until he or she finally shapes up, but it is rather a promise to work together toward a mutual goal, a higher state.

This is not meant to advocate a utopia where leaders and followers somehow merge into one happy, loving, homogeneous group. Nor is it to say that people in leadership positions who love their subordinates will automatically be great leaders. However, without the ability to love, it is impossible to be a great, and perhaps not even a good, leader.

The relationship between the leader and follower is most closely analogous to that between parent and child. The good parent listens to his or her child and considers both the child's desires and abilities along with outside demands and personal responsibilities before making a decision. Whenever possible, that decision is explained. Also, the good parent will strive to set a good example for the child, to be someone whose personal integrity, courage, and competence are worth emulating.

In both love and leadership, perception is frequently as important as reality. If one is perceived as a good leader, one who acts out of love, then the recipient of that leadership and love normally will react by both offering loyalty and returning that love. The possibility of successfully faking it, of making the perception different from the reality, increases with distance.

An absent grandparent, for instance, who is careful never to miss a birthday or Christmas is perceived as loving by a grandchild. Likewise, employees of a large, multilocation organization rarely see the CEO or president of their organization; fewer still ever actually talk with him or her. Yet every employee has an opinion about that person based on a few significant factors.

This intangible assessment of top management, largely emotional, is based on a combination of 1) the reputation the boss built on the way up, 2) the individual employee's knowledge or perception of the performance of the leader in his or her current job, and 3) the individual employee's perception of how well the organization is "taking care" of her or him. It is important because it translates into tangible performance, how readily employees follow the CEO or president and give that extra effort when asked. When this assessment is sufficiently positive, employees have been known to brag about the virtues of their chief executive.

In fact, the CEO or president may be doing little personally to see that the employees' physical and mental welfare is being attended to. He or she may not even be "setting the tone" but may be blessed, accidentally or intentionally, with a good staff who create the aura of proficiency and caring. The results will be the same.

Similarly, a child will profess love for both grandparents—since both have been signing the cards that come with the gifts. Yet, it is possible that left to her own devices, grandma might never admit that she has grandchildren, let alone remember their birthdays.

A historical example is seen in Napoleon. His men loved him, as demonstrated by their statements and actions. Yet Napoleon's cavalier attitude toward them was summed up in his claim that he had "an income of 20,000 men a month to spend." His troops didn't know his opinion of them. They knew only that he had led them to glory and satisfied both their physical and mental needs and desires.

In Napoleon's case, he lavished all his love and attention on his immediate staff. As long as these people felt loved, they passed the feeling on to the lower levels. It is possible for a CEO or president to do the same.

The reverse is also possible. A leader may be an extremely talented technician with a high regard for his or her people, but if that feeling is not made known to the employees, he or she might not have their support at all. Without a capable staff—the filter through which nonmanagement employees and most of the management personnel see their CEO or president—the positive impact of that executive will be minimal.

Looking again at the parallel case of grandparent and grandchild, a grandmother's deep love for her grandchildren will not be recognized if she is unable to acknowledge special occasions, can never visit, and/or is being presented in a bad light by grandpa, parents, and other relatives—her "staff."

As the distance is decreased, the concepts of love and leadership become more obviously intertwined. Department heads, while laying the groundwork for the reputations that will follow them throughout their careers, must truly love their people if they wish to be known as good leaders. If they bring technical expertise and ambition but no warmth to their position, the employees will return the investment in kind. Subordinates may do precisely as told, but they will not give the extra effort that is the mark of the well-led.

Another similarity between love and leadership is willingness to forgive. Ongoing faults will be overlooked or compensated for; mistakes will be tolerated and not held against the perpetrator. It goes both ways. Many a young manager has been saved because his or her subordinates "covered" an error. Such behavior is no accident, just as it is no accident when adjacent departments choose not to cover for their managers. In the former case, love is being returned in full.

What makes all this threatening to many executives—young and old—is that it involves taking an enormous chance. Unfortunately, loving employees isn't enough by itself. Just as the object of one's romantic love may not always be swept off his or her feet on schedule, so too in the leading-led relationship. As a result, an executive might find herself or himself a victim of unrequited love on a grand scale. Avoiding that outcome depends in part on competence. There must be substance to an individual's performance or the verdict is likely to be, "Well, he's a nice guy, but ..."

The leader who combines the ability to love and be loved with technical knowledge and dedication will rise to the top. Such a leader makes an active effort to ensure that both the physical and mental welfare of those placed under his or her responsibility are taken care of—and that those people know it. The leader who blends the emotional and rational elements of leadership is the stuff that legends are made of.

Axiom #**19** *Love is what makes leadership work; it is what makes the difference between manipulating people and leading people. You cannot manipulate people into doing quality work.*

20 Outreach
Seek Answers Outside the Castle Keep

*T*he kingdom was behaving oddly. That much was obvious to the king. He just could not put his finger on the problem. It particularly bothered him that none of his top officials seemed to be as worried as he was.

So he called a meeting to ask his royal advisers for their help. "Something seems to be wrong," he announced at the beginning of the meeting. "When we look down from our tower (the king meant himself, but he was a devotee of the royal "we"), we never see anyone smiling. People look shabby. And we don't get visitors to our court anymore. What's going on?"

Silence fell at the table. After waiting in vain several long, painful minutes for a response, the king sighed. "All right, we'll just start here at our right," he prompted, "and go around the table. We want to hear each of your theories about what's going on."

The Duke of Operations (who now regretted having come to the meeting room 30 minutes early so as to make sure he got the seat immediately to the king's right) stood and said, "I agree that something seems wrong, your majesty, but I'm afraid I can offer nothing more definitive. Operations have been a little sluggish for the last quarter or two, but I am sure that it is just part of a natural cycle. We are, of course, hampered by the people and materials we are given. I can assure you I will order all my people to work harder."

The next to speak was the Earl of Human Resources. "I, too, have been of a mind that something is wrong, your majesty, so I had one of my people do some checking in the records," stated the Earl. "It seems we are getting a much higher percentage of people who are not native to our fair land. In addition, there have been some professional agitators causing trouble. If it weren't for these factors we can't control, everything would be great, I feel certain."

The king obviously was not pleased by what he had heard so far, which made the Knight of Training even more uncomfortable as he stood. "Well, we're doing everything we can with the budget we've got," he apologized with obvious defensiveness. "I presented a very good training plan at the last budget hearings, but the plan was positively gutted. We've had to cut back virtually everything except executive attendance at conferences."

The head of Finance was, of course, a Count. "Well," he pronounced, "I don't know what's wrong out there, but I can tell you that money is flowing the wrong way in here. It hasn't shown up on the annual statement yet because we were able to do a little creative bookkeeping the last few years—wrote off some of the old training facilities and the like—but it can't continue."

The king almost spoke up because he had never realized that the black ink used to write the budget/expenditures report was magical in origin. He made a note to read the next report a lot more carefully.

And so it went around the table. Everyone agreed with the king that something was wrong, but they were all sure that their department was blameless, and no one had anything to contribute as a solution. The meeting was adjourned with nothing resolved.

That night during supper, the king was telling the queen about the frustrating meeting. On the spur-of-the-moment, he asked the maid who was in the process of clearing the table, "Young lady, what is wrong in this kingdom?"

The maid almost dropped the dishes she was holding when she realized that the king was speaking to her (the term "young lady" had ceased being appropriate for the queen some years previous). She began with a strong voice, "Well, the way I see it . . ." and then she remembered who and where she was. She started over. "Well, I am very happy here, your highness," she said and all but ran from the room.

"This isn't going to be easy," said the king. "We know there is something wrong, but no one in this castle will tell us what it is."

"Why don't you go outside the castle, then?" asked the queen.

"A splendid idea," said the king. "We'll do it tomorrow."

Sure enough, the next morning the king dressed in his finest garb and, accompanied by a ceremonial guard, a palace artist, and three secretaries, the king went out to ask the "little people" what was wrong with the kingdom. He thought it amazing that they found 23 consecutive people who thought everything was fine and who loved living in the kingdom. (It had looked as if the string might be broken at 17 when one teenager was frowning as he began to answer, but then his mother arrived and he spoke of his happiness instead.)

"How'd it go?" asked the queen that night at dinner.

"Not well," answered the king. "Nobody would talk to us. You'd think they'd never talked to a king before."

Suddenly it occurred to him that what he had just said was very true. The people had never had the opportunity to speak to the king before. If he really wanted to find out what they thought of the kingdom, he decided, he would have to go in disguise.

He spent the next three days on his own, roaming his land. The castle public relations wizard was told to announce that the king was ill and would not be seeing anyone. All of his appointments were cancelled or shifted.

The result was the greatest learning experience of his life— once he learned to listen more and to debate and defend less. By and large, the residents did enjoy living in the kingdom, but they were worried about the future, and many had already begun investigating moving to another kingdom where prospects looked brighter.

They confirmed what he had already guessed from the comments of his royal advisers—that no one person or department was totally to blame. They added a second thought, however, that everyone was to blame to some degree. And then they gave him a great number of specific ideas on how to improve things. Many of the ideas they could do by themselves, with royal permission of course.

The king astounded the executive court at the next meeting with his recommendations. He amazed them even further when he announced his new order for them. "From henceforth," he said, "each month, each of you will spend one day outside these walls actually talking to people. On the first of each month, you will be assigned a small town or a section of our capital city to visit. You will go there in plain garb and spend at least eight hours talking with people about the kingdom. Within 48 hours after your return, you will report directly to me about what you have learned and what your recommendations are. We, that is to say, I (there was an audible gasp) will do the same. That will undoubtedly make our meetings more productive. Incidentally, if you miss a month, you'll be on probation. If you miss two months, you'll be out of a job. Any questions?"

Henceforth, the kingdom flourished.

Axiom #**20** *Intending to talk to "real people" is often not enough by itself. Outreach may call for a specific plan—with a detailed structure—to force executives to get out of the executive suite and interact with different layers of the company. This is especially true at the beginning of a quality process.*

21 *Paradigms*

The Middle Management Dilemma: How to Live with Quality

*F*ran and R. J. started work at Smith Inc. on the same day. In fact, they first met at New Employee Orientation Hour and became fast friends. They worked in different departments, but their responsibilities were similar.

Both were excited to start their first "real job." In fact, during that first week, they both thought of several things that they thought could be done better in their respective departments. It seemed a little presumptuous to be offering advice at that early stage, and probably neither one alone would have had the nerve to approach a middle manager with those ideas, but they egged each other on.

And they both got the same response: "Yeah. Right. Look, we do things the way we do things around here because this is the way we do things around here. What's more, I like the way we do things; it's always been plenty good for me and it keeps the boss happy. But, tell you what, you look like a bright, eager, sincere young person. Why don't you take notes about things you'd like to see changed around here? And you keep that notebook to yourself as you work hard and keep your nose clean. Maybe in a dozen years or so, you can take over this job. And then you can do it your way. Until then, we do it my way. Questions?"

Neither had any questions. But after a couple of long discussions, both decided to follow the suggestion and keep the notebooks. Both liked the company, and they intended to make their work at Smith Inc. their careers.

Keeping the notebooks came to be something they did as a matter of course. Nobody else knew about them, and perhaps without each other's determination, both might have abandoned the project.

As luck would have it, they were both promoted to middle management at the same time.

As Fran and R. J. were settling into their respective desks on their first day in their new jobs—just as they were reaching for their well-worn "My Way" notebooks—a memo was dropped into each of their "In" baskets. It was from Mr. Smith himself (well, actually, it was Smith III, who was the current Smith) and it said, "As we launch our quality effort this week, I just want to remind everyone in management once again: Be sure to turn to your employees for their ideas. They know things that we in management do not."

The first thought that crossed both minds was, "What about my 'My Way' notebook?"

R. J. was so mad that little productive work got done that day. Fran found a notice for a new training class titled "Middle Managers and Mid-Career Crisis: Who Said THEY Could Think?" on the bulletin board in the hallway and signed up immediately.

When Fran told R. J. about the course that evening on the way home (they had been car-pooling for over 10 years), R. J. wasn't interested. "Listen," R. J. said, "I've got it figured out. I'll go ahead and have some of those quality teams that everyone is so hot about, but I'll tell 'em what to work on . . . the ideas in my 'My Way' notebook."

Fran agreed that it might work but tried to talk R. J. into taking the course anyway. It was to no avail.

The course was interesting—all about changing roles from being a minidictator (no matter how much fun it was) to being more of a coach and a teacher and a cheerleader and a resource and, most of all, a leader.

At the first meeting between Fran and the department team leaders, Fran offered the "My Way" notebook as a possible resource—she even told about how it got started and how the quality process had kind of put it in limbo. Everyone had a good laugh together over a couple of the older ideas that really sounded a bit silly now—and found one that still looked pretty good. "I'll leave this thing on the table outside my office," Fran said. "If you want to use it, feel free."

Meanwhile, R. J. was at war. Quality teams in R. J.'s area were given specific ideas from R. J.'s "My Way" book to evaluate. Recommendations for implementation were expected promptly, but there were always delays for one reason or another.

Fran and R. J. began to avoid talking about the quality process while driving back and forth to work. Both of them found it difficult to stay off the topic, but Fran hated listening to R. J. complain, and Fran's enthusiasm was too much for R. J. After Fran mentioned that "There have been 15 ideas from my 'My Way' book that have evolved into implemented actions . . . although I barely recognized some of them," they tacitly agreed to declare the topic of the quality process off limits. None of R. J.'s ideas had been implemented yet.

The car pool finally fell apart when Fran was promoted.

Axiom #21 *Middle managers do have a unique problem with most quality processes. There is no getting around the fact that the role of middle managers will undergo a classic paradigm shift from being directors and micromanagers to being coaches and resources. This new model provides appealing opportunities for cooperation and innovation.*

22 *Performance*
A Diatribe on Quality (and Non-Quality)

*I*n the spring of 1987, an American consumer (one of the authors) decided to "buy American" when in the market for a new lawn mower. He chose an American company that used a well-known

American-made engine, a company that he knew had a formal quality process in place.

After less than two months of use, the engine blew up, thoroughly startling the consumer's teenage son, who was pushing it at the time. It took the customer relations department at the mower company and its supplier, the engine-maker, over six weeks to decide that repairing the problem was their responsibility. It took another week to provide a short block to the repair facility.

As summer heated up, so did the consumer. The repaired mower worked once, with difficulty. The consumer returned to the phone and requested an additional repair. Thus began near-daily calls to the manufacturer's customer representative, who finally agreed that such a repair was in order. But the repair, the consumer was told, would take several weeks to arrange.

The consumer shifted ground; he requested a full refund. The company found the request unbelievable. The consumer was assured by both the customer service representative and the head of the company's quality process that the company made a wonderful product and that the quality process assured that it would continue to do so—complete with impressive statistics. The consumer explained that he was not interested in their statistics, he wanted them to listen to *his* numbers: He was one-for-one—every product he had ever purchased from them had failed.

Stuck with the option of waiting several weeks for further repair (the customer service rep told him several times that he, the customer rep, could not authorize a refund), the consumer called the president of the company. He began with a description of all of his dealings with the company's products and people, and reiterated his desire for a full refund so that he could "buy a Japanese mower."

That's when the conversation took a turn toward the bizarre. Far from being conciliatory, the company president appeared to feel abused. He also seemed to be confused as to who was the provider and who was the customer. His exact words were, "Well, you must really have a quality problem if you treat your customers the same way you are treating me!" The consumer responded that in this particular instance *he* was the customer.

The company president agreed to a refund and, roughly three weeks later, the consumer was informed that when he delivered his broken lawn mower to the nearest company service center (62 miles from his home and closed on Saturdays), he could pick up his refund check.

The bottom line? The company was out all the money it originally received and had custody of a thoroughly defective lawn mower. It had an angry ex-customer who not only will never buy another product from them, but who is also bound and determined to tell anyone who will listen about the company's deficient products and services.

What other options did the company have? Assuming that all the statistics that the consumer kept hearing were true, it is probably fair to say that the lawn mower he had was, indeed, a "lemon." The minute it became obvious to the customer service rep that there really was a problem, the customer should have been offered a new mower. If nothing else, the cloud of smoke that had enveloped the teenager when the engine exploded demonstrated that this was no ordinary situation.

A new mower should have then been delivered to the consumer's house that weekend with a request to retrieve the "bad" mower for "study." (Suggested statement: "Sonovagun, so that's where the bad one went! We were afraid that we had let one bad one slip through this year. Boy, am I glad you helped us find it.") The consumer would have been reassured that the company regretted the inconvenience and that it was determined to find out what went wrong so that it could further improve its already excellent product.

What would the bottom line have been then? The company would still have had possession of a bum mower, and it would have "spent" a new mower, but it would have retained the profit from the old mower. In addition, it would have had an advocate in the consumer market who would look to it first when shopping for any other product that it makes.

Perhaps more importantly in terms of its quality process, this scenario would have sent a powerful message throughout the organization. If, in addition, the president had publicly congratulated the customer service rep for his astute and innovative handling of the situation, it would have validated the president's support of the widely published "quality goals" of the company, a clear act of leadership.

The second-best solution (since the customer service rep obviously did not feel that he had the authority to make such a commitment) would have been for the president to jump into the fray on the side of the consumer and personally arrange the delivery of the new mower. As it was, his attitude and actions demonstrated very clearly that quality and customer service were secondary to winning arguments.

Axiom #22 *Unless a company leadership team is prepared to back up its statements and slogans with quality performance, the money spent on halfhearted quality programs should be invested in enlarging the customer complaint department.*

23 Perseverance
The Ghost of Programs Past

"**B**ah!" the company president said. "We don't need some complicated program or process or whatever to whip this company into shape. We just need for somebody around here to have a couple of good ideas to improve quality, and we'll be right back into the thick of it. I'll make the announcement myself tomorrow that we expect everyone to work smarter and contribute more."

Having brought the staff meeting to an abrupt close, he decided he'd had enough for one day. So he told his secretary to cancel all of his appointments for the rest of the afternoon, and he went home. Even if the house was lonely, at least it would be quiet, and he wouldn't have to listen to any more money-eating theories on how to pull the company out of its little slump.

Once home, there wasn't much to do. In his case, "business" and "life" were pretty much interchangeable. He couldn't even remember the last time he'd taken a Saturday off, much less a midweek afternoon. "Perhaps a nap will get rid of this headache," he decided.

The couch welcomed him and he fell quickly and very soundly asleep.

He thought he heard the hallway clock strike three—which struck him as vaguely surprising since he didn't have a hallway clock. A sad-looking man in a conservative business suit appeared next to the couch, standing about a foot and a half above the floor.

"Who are you? How did you get in here? And how do you do that?" the company president asked, looking at the space between the man's feet and the rug. To his own surprise, he didn't seem all that upset. In fact, he didn't even bother to sit up.

"Well, this is going to sound a little out of date," the strange man said, "but I am the Ghost of Programs Past."

"You're kidding."

"No, seriously, I'm here to remind you of some of the programs you've run at your company over the past couple of decades and what glorious failures they were," said the strange man. "Here's the uncomfortable part. You have to hold my hand so we can go on a little trip together."

The company president couldn't really tell if he got up from the couch or not, but he did take the man's hand (he figured he had better; maybe the guy had a gun), and he did have a sensation of traveling.

When they stopped, the place looked familiar. "Hey, this is my company—but it looks like it did 25 years ago. What have you done to everyone?" the company president asked.

"Nothing. You see, it *is* 25 years ago, and no one can see us or hear us, but we can hear them. Care to listen to those two over there?" They floated over to a water cooler where two young men were talking to each other.

"Well, I finally got an answer back on that suggestion I put in the suggestion box," said the first.

"Oh, what did they say?" replied the second.

"That they are considering it and that they thank me for submitting it."

"When did you submit it?"

"Let's see . . . this is July . . . it was right after Christmas . . . about six months ago, I guess."

"Yeah, that's about par for the course around here. I submitted an idea once. Got a flat 'No' back about six months later. Haven't bothered playing that game again."

"What do you think of that?" the strange man asked the company president.

"Smart aleck kid, doesn't he realize that the management committee has lots of other things to do beside look at his wacky ideas? There's a business to run," answered the company president. "That kid looks familiar, but I don't think he works for me."

"He should look familiar," the strange man said. "He's your primary competitor nowadays. But, come on, we have a couple more stops to make."

Again, the sensation of traveling. Again, a familiar-looking surrounding—his building, but not quite as long ago.

"Now what?" said the company president.

"Remember those three folks over there?" said the strange man. "They're that high-priced consultant team you brought in to study efficiency and design work."

"Oh, yes, I didn't see their stopwatches at first," said the company president. "They did a lot of good work for us. They were expensive as all get-out, but we sure changed a thing or two around here."

"I suggest you go listen to the two workers who are standing over by the water cooler this time," the strange man sighed.

"Do you believe this crap?" said the first one.

"What's the problem? Those sounded like fairly good ideas

to me," said the second. "It's not like we couldn't do things a little better around here."

"Yeah, I know, but look at these proposals. Don't they look just a little bit familiar to you? Half this stuff is what we told them at that not-for-attribution meeting they held, and the other half is stuff you and I have talked about a dozen times. Now I know what 'not-for-attribution' means. It means they aren't going to share the credit. Have you heard what those guys get paid?"

"Well, if they knew so darn much," said the company president, "why didn't they speak up?"

"How?" asked the strange man. "Through the suggestion box?"

"No, we gave them opportunities. Lots of opportunities. My door was always open."

"Let's take a look at those opportunities, shall we?"

More traveling sensation. Same location.

"Looks familiar," observed the company president. "This wouldn't be today would it?"

"It is."

"Shouldn't I have a new ghost or something?" queried the company president.

"Don't worry, I've been cross-trained, and this is sort of a gray area, anyway," replied the specter.

"I'll take your word for it. Now what?" asked the company president.

"Remember that 'An Idea Every Hour' program you just finished? The one that went on for a whole month and urged employees to submit ideas on how to improve things? You remember, the one with the coffee cups and all that stuff? Well, this is the first day after."

"Let me guess. I should go listen to the two young ladies at the water cooler."

"You catch on fast."

"You're not going to believe this," a scornful voice proclaimed. "Last night, on the way home, I thought of a great idea on how to save a whole bunch of time in our department. I was so excited about it, I even wrote it down as soon as I got home. My husband thought I was crazy. So I came in this morning and went up to my boss with my big idea. Know what he said?"

"I'm afraid to ask," answered the second.

"He said, 'You're too late, the Idea Every Hour thing is over.' So I said, 'Okay, so I don't get a coffee cup or a trip to Hawaii. It's still a good idea and it would help out.' He said, 'Look we haven't got time to look at it. We're going to be swamped for the next several months trying to look at that big stack of harebrained ideas that we already got. Get back to work.' Do you believe that?"

"Around here? Sure. I'm just surprised they thought we were smart for a month."

"Are you getting the point?" the strange man asked. "Your employees have all sorts of ideas on how to improve things, but you're going to have to quit making it so hard for them to contribute. Well, I think I've given you enough to think about for now. Let's get you home."

"Wait a minute, don't I at least get a visit from some friend of yours who is going to show me my company's future?" asked the company president as he realized he was back in his living room.

"My friend, if you haven't already learned enough from our time together, your company doesn't have a future."

Axiom $^{\#}$**23** *The failure of past efforts can provide valuable clues as to a future course of action. In this case, programs to improve quality failed to establish a structure that enabled employees to actively participate on an ongoing basis. Learn your lessons from past experience and persevere—even in the absence of a supernatural phenomenon goading you to action.*

24 Priorities
How's That Again?

Customers are easier to deal with than employees.
You can hang up on customers.

Axiom #**24** *Once.*

25 *Reality*

Three Myths Concerning Quality

As quality processes became more popular in the United States during the 1980s, several myths developed that passed as "common knowledge." The popularity of at least three of these myths can be attributed to their usefulness in enabling leaders to rationalize delaying effective efforts to improve quality. These three things that "everyone knows" are quite a deterrent to action:

Myth #1 *"Quality processes are for fixing problems. Only companies in real trouble need these tools; solid companies are better advised to direct their energies elsewhere."*

The opposite is far closer to the truth. Companies in trouble are likely to have a crisis mentality, including a large percentage of recalcitrant skeptics. This is no time to attempt to institute a culture change. Quality processes are more likely to be successful in healthy companies that are trying to move from a sound competitive position to dominance in their field: quality is for taking advantage of and creating opportunities. It is true that these same tools can solve problems, but for every Xerox and Ford Motor Company that fights its way back from the brink of disaster, there are dozens of companies whose patience and/or fiscal pockets will be insufficient to make it possible for them to survive if they wait too long to focus on quality.

Myth #2 *"American service quality efforts are 'primitive.' Smart companies will wait until the bugs are out of service quality before committing resources."*

If this were true, why are the odds of having an enjoyable time at an amusement park or an edible fast-food meal or an accurate bank statement noticeably higher than the odds of getting a hassle-free, American-made automobile? All have complex systems of producing and delivering a final product, but the service folks are much more likely to meet expectations. Quality processes are appropriate for, and can have a positive impact on, any group of humans with a common purpose—be they in manufacturing, entertainment, financial services, health care, government, education, or any other field. There is no excuse not to make the effort, even in service.

Myth #3 *"It takes too long for a quality process to bear any fruit."*

It does take several years for a quality process and the cultural changes that inevitably accompany it to become firmly entrenched. Positive results, however, begin immediately. Employees are invariably eager to address long-standing problems if given the opportunity, and some improvement can be expected from the outset. Waiting to begin a quality process because it takes a long time for it to fully mature is illogical. Time is slipping by. As recently as the 1970s, an adequate question for predicting business success was "Who's any good?" In the 1980s, the question that more fully judged capabilities was "Who's getting better?" The question for the 1990s is even more sophisticated: "Who is getting better faster?" Those left at the starting gate waiting for the ideal time to start improving quality will soon be so far behind the leaders as to be inconsequential.

Axiom #25 *Look beyond pervasive myths about quality. Many myths garner their popularity because they provide an excuse for inactivity. The reality is that there is no time like the present for beginning a quality process.*

26 *Requisites*
Beyond Lip Service: An Action Plan for Top Management

*Q*uality by exhortation is a short-term approach that sows the seeds of its own destruction; long-term quality demands much more. It is not enough to assure employees that, "This time I'm serious. No, I mean it, really serious. We're going to become a company obsessed with quality. I will consider it a personal failure if we don't."

No matter how heartfelt the sentiment, when top management limits its pursuit of quality to rousing statements and good intentions, employees will do the same. What is needed is not lip service but action—starting with managers who invest the requisite time, ego, and effort.

The rank and file notice how top managers spend their time. Taking time to learn about quality underscores commitment to it. Any manager can become a bit of an expert on the topic by reading up on the subject and by attending a seminar or two. Maybe a visit to other companies with a reputation for doing things right would also be in order.

Taking time to talk to others about quality is another powerful signal, important for reasons of both style and substance. When the word gets on the corporate grapevine that the boss is spending valuable time talking to people—at all levels—about quality, the message will be clear that quality has a high priority. Concurrently, by engaging in these conversations, an executive learns a great deal more about the company and about the concerns of employees.

Taking time to define a quality process for the organization is also time well spent. By making sure that a process is uniquely fitted to their organization, top managers make it easier for everyone to make quality a part of what they do as a matter of course.

Defining the procedures for participation in an organization's quality process must be done in the main by the top management of the company for several reasons. If the top executives simply turn it over to a midmanagement team to work out the details ("We'll approve whatever you say"), their own commitment will always be in doubt. If they hire a consultant group to do the job ("They've done it before, so they'll know best"), the process will always be known—and seen—as the consultants' process. When the consultants leave, so will the heart of the process. The more effective long-term alternative is to form a Quality Steering Committee to define the organization's quality process.

The commitment of time—the most precious thing an executive contributes to an organization—will be heavy at first. A Quality Steering Committee, depending on the size of the company, can require weekly meetings for a period of several months. This is in addition to the time needed for reading, thinking, and discussions outside of meetings.

Once a process is defined and launched, the time requirement on the executives will be reduced. It will be "limited" to staying abreast of the process in the organization, keeping up with developments in the ever-evolving field of quality, taking part in such things as recognition ceremonies, occasional (e.g., monthly) meetings of the Quality Steering Committee, and, once the process is an obvious success, speaking engagements to aid other organizations, especially suppliers.

Top managers must also participate in the process itself. The quality process design is where time and ego intersect. The most effective way to convince employees that top managers are personally involved in quality is to design a quality process that calls for identical responses from all levels of employees. A well-defined 100 percent employee involvement quality process is not for the timid. It calls for optimism and courage on the part of top management; it assumes that everyone on the payroll will play an active role.

The litmus test for determining how serious top managers are about quality is simple: Whose behavior changes? It is not nearly enough to direct changes in others' behavior in the name of quality; the top managers' personal behavior also must change . . . and the entire company should know about it.

A top manager leading an organization into a quality process will have to be highly visible. This is no time to be shy. When a top manager does something positive to improve quality, the word must get out. Being active is not enough by itself; being obvious is also necessary.

By working to improve his or her personal contribution, a top manager becomes better able to appreciate what everyone else in the company is up against when they attempt to make changes. It also gives him or her something to talk about on the elevator with whomever else is there.

The most personally enjoyable demonstration of commitment that an executive can make is to be actively involved in the programs of recognition, gratitude, and celebration that are part and parcel of a well-defined quality process. Ceremonies to congratulate employees should command a significant portion of the executive's time.

Again, reasons of both style and substance come into play. By taking part, by talking with and thanking the people who have done well, the top manager once again indicates the level of importance that he or she attaches to the process. And, once again, by listening to the winners describe why they are being thanked, he or she can learn what is going on inside the organization.

Top level executives who make this personal commitment play a vital role in a quality process. Without their involvement, any quality process will fall far short of potential.

Axiom #**26** *The personal commitment of top management is absolutely essential to the success of a quality process.*

27 Resources
Allocating Time, Money, and Materials for a Quality Process

*T*he eye-catching title of the best-selling book *Quality Is Free*, by Phil Crosby, was not deliberately misleading. A quality process consumes resources in several forms. Crosby only meant that any quality effort more than pays for itself in the long run.

Time is the most obvious investment. Besides their own time, top management commits thousands of hours of their employees' time. A company of 1000 people, for instance, that encourages employees to meet as quality teams for 30 minutes each week is committing 500 hours a week to its own improvement. Training in quality methods also requires time. Happily, one of the by-products of improving quality is increased efficiency and effectiveness—in short, a savings of time.

Direct expenditures are also part of the investment. These include the costs associated with hiring consultants, adding to the payroll an appropriate staff to run the process from day to day, building and maintaining a set of training courses, and designing and implementing a program of recognition, gratitude, and celebration, as well as capital expenditures arising from quality decisions. Are all of these expenditures necessary?

Comedian Steven Wright maintains that, "Everything is within walking distance ... if you have the time." In the same sense, no one really needs to ever hire a consultant because any staff of intelligent people could, with no outside help, design a workable quality process ... if they wanted to take the time. Consultants can, however, save a person or an organization many hours of research and prevent reinventing the wheel.

To best capitalize on the expense of hiring consultants, the trick is to use them as "consultants," not as sources of the "one true way." An organization can bring them in, agree to a short-term contract that includes the consultant leaving behind (with no strings attached) everything that is developed or purchased, and proceed to drain them of all useful information before showing them to the door.

Someone *does* have to run the quality process from day to day; somebody's career should rise or fall with the success of the process. Unless the organization is very small (less than 50 people), a full-time position is in order. This should not, however, become a mini-empire. For example, at the Paul Revere Insurance Group, the quality process for 3000-plus people is administered by 5 people. For comparison's sake, before the new CEO, James Broadhead, dismantled it in 1990, the quality department for Florida Power and Light—a company of 9000-plus people—numbered in excess of 100.

The job of running the quality process is considered by those who have held it to be the second-best job in the company—second only to that of president or CEO. The energy level, the constant innovations, the continuous effort to improve everything possible can be a great deal of fun. It is also satisfying to know that you are contributing to a way for hundreds, if not thousands, of individuals to gain control over a significant portion of their lives while simultaneously making the organization stronger and more profitable.

Training is not optional. Depending on the size and experience of the training department, it may choose to either develop its own courses to support the quality process or to purchase "off-the-shelf" courses and adapt them as appropriate. As with the development of the process as a whole, care must be taken to insure that the training courses are perceived to be "owned" by the trainers and the company.

An investment in training—which includes both the training staff and the courses themselves—can be reduced significantly if the organization buys complete rights to any material purchased from a vendor. Such an arrangement makes it possible for the organization to change or update the course as lessons are learned and the quality process evolves. It also avoids going through the annual ritual of buying new copies of old books for $200 each and having to "renew the site fee."

Capital expenditures as a result of ideas that come out of a quality process are to be judged on their own merits, not indulged just because they are "Quality Ideas." In some organizations, a percentage of funds saved by previous quality ideas is turned over to the quality process director for discretionary use as a way to fund particularly attractive ideas quickly.

The last category—recognition, gratitude, and celebration— is a more controversial investment. The essential focus of such a program is to say thank you, not to act as an incentive. When employees take on additional responsibilities they *deserve* to be recognized. Yes, it will take time to say thank you in a frequent and timely manner. Yes, it will cost as much as $50 to $100 per person per year to fund a program that says thank you to all deserving people in ways both symbolic and material. But, as with every other aspect of expenditure in a quality process, it is a proven investment.

There is a standard joke in corporate America that it is tough to stay focused on draining the swamp when you constantly find yourself up to your hips in alligators. Investment in a quality process is an investment in draining the swamp; maintaining the investment is the promise to owners, employees, and customers that the alligator population will steadily decrease.

Axiom $^\#$**27** *Be prepared for an initial outlay to cover quality-related expenditures. Time, materials, and expertise must be paid for. After start-up costs, however, a quality process will more than cover its own expenses. Quality professionals conservatively estimate that a well-run quality process yields a minimum of a 5-to-1 return on investment.*

28 Responsibility
Who Does What
in a "Black Box" Model

*E*ffective leadership has been compared to a "black box" where the leader's responsibility is to ensure that whatever goes into the box—people, resources, information—is sufficient to produce what is expected to come out of the box. The details of what goes on inside the box are of concern only if the output does not measure up or if there is reason to believe that actions inside the box violate ethical or professional standards.

Responsibility for the work in the box rests on the shoulders of those doing the work. It is appropriate for the leader to ask for periodic updates on what is happening in the box to check the status of projects under his or her umbrella; and sometimes the leader is invited into the box to give advice or help solve a problem, but even then, caution is advisable. Leaders at all levels do well to remember that their proper concern lies with directing overall strategy for their subordinates, not with defining specifics of how a particular assignment is carried out.

In the 1991 Gulf War, General Norman Schwarzkopf (USA) became an instant folk hero to Americans, and a very real hero to his military subordinates, by practicing black box leadership. One of his subordinates was General Walt Boomer (USMC), a Marine who was responsible for the right flank (made up of two Marine divisions) of the allied forces. Schwarzkopf explained to Boomer what he expected from the Marine forces and, after conferring with his staff, Boomer returned with three alternatives. At the end of the presentation of each of the three possibilities, Schwarzkopf simply said, "Yes, that would work."

It is almost certain that "Stormin' Norman" had a preference among Boomer's three plans (and some thoughts on how to improve it), but he refused the opportunity to choose among the three. The attack on the right was Boomer's responsibility; therefore Boomer had to have the authority to do it the way that he judged to be the best. Similar restraint is possible, and necessary, in any management position in business. It isn't easy; the temptation to meddle can border on overwhelming. It takes an enormous amount of will power—and trust—to not meddle in the details of a subordinate's job.

The advantage to black box leadership is clear. Only because Schwarzkopf allowed Boomer to truly own the process for which he was responsible was Boomer able to react confidently to the constantly changing situation. Precious moments—or days—are lost if subordinates feel obligated to play "Mother, may I?" games whenever there is need for a change to a detailed plan that they have been asked to carry out.

In practicing black box leadership, General Schwarzkopf was in step with an approach to leadership that is not only found throughout military history but is also coming back into vogue at high levels in the Department of Defense. In the mid-1980s, the assistant secretary of defense for installations sent a compact package to commanding officers of military installations taking part in a program called "Model Installations." The package included a wallet-size "rule book," a five-page manual for installation operation (which replaced a 380-page handbook), and a one-page directive on installation management. The card defined the inputs and outcomes expected from this black box approach:

MODEL INSTALLATIONS:
AN EXPERIMENT IN DEREGULATION

Commanders run their bases their way,
rather than Washington's way

- Model Installations will
  - strive for excellence
  - try new methods, risk failures
  - use any savings to improve the installation
  - put up with visitors
- Headquarters will
  - help model commanders quickly get the authority they need
  - try not to run bases or second guess commanders
  - protect planned budget, without pouring money in or skimming savings away
  - find out and publicize what's happening

EXCELLENT INSTALLATIONS:
THE FOUNDATION OF DEFENSE

The essence of black box leadership is that the leader believes that virtually every subordinate (at any level), given the opportunity, training, and support, will make an honest effort to do a good job. In addition, the leader believes that decisions made closer to the action are made faster and better. It may be more viscerally satisfying to put aside the responsibility of leading and to get down in the trenches where the action is, but good leaders know that they cannot afford to get caught up in inappropriate details.

Axiom #**28** *The black box approach to leadership means delegating to subordinates without meddling in the details. It does not mean that a leader is off the hook; the leader is still responsible for what goes into the box and for the results that come out.*

29 Self-Confidence
When Picking a Consultant, Be Sure the Fit Is Right

One day, Mr. Brown decided that in order to present a better image to the world around him he needed a new suit. Being a man of some means, he immediately went to the men's store that had the reputation for being the finest men's clothier in the city.

He was greeted at the door by an elegantly dressed salesman who spoke in an affected French accent, "Good day, monsieur, may I be of any assistance to you?"

Mr. Brown said, "Yes, I would like a new suit, preferably a suit with—" That was as much as Mr. Brown was able to say before the salesman said, "You have come to exactly zee right place. Let me assure you zat we can provide you with exactly what you need. Please come zis way."

Mr. Brown was led over to a display rack that held some very fine suits. He spotted one that appeared to be just what he wanted, but before he could take it off the rack, the salesman handed him another saying, "Here you are, monsieur. I sink zis will provide you with just the look you are seeking."

Mr. Brown conceded to himself that the suit the salesman was handing him did seem quite nice so he took it into the dressing room and tried it on. The salesman told him it looked marvelous.

"I'm not sure," Mr. Brown said. "The trousers do fit perfectly, but do you see here how the left sleeve seems to be a little short?"

"Did you notice," the salesman said, "zee material? It not only looks but feels wonderful. Perhaps if you flexed your arm just a little? Zere, I knew zat would do it."

"Well, yes, but when I do, it doesn't seem to fit on my right shoulder very well."

"Did I mention," the salesman asked, "zat zee lapels are zee very latest style. Did you notice zeem on the mayor at zee awards banquet last week? All zee fashion setters had lapels just like zose. Could you roll your shoulder forward just a little?"

"I do like the fashion, quite attractive, and I have heard nothing but good things about your store here, but when I roll my shoulder to make it fit better, it seems a little short down the right side."

"Besides our well-earned reputation, you may not have heard about our discount for first-time buyers. Zee color, she is perfect on you. Lean to your right just a little."

Anxious to be known as someone who shopped at the most exclusive men's store in town, Mr. Brown paid for the suit and decided to wear it home rather than change back into his old suit.

As he walked down the sidewalk, he passed two older women. "Oh," the first said, "did you see that poor man? All bent over like that from arthritis. How he must suffer!"

"Yes," said the other, "but what a marvelous tailor he must have. Did you notice how nicely his suit fit?"

Axiom #**29** *Asking for help with a quality process can be a real shortcut, but don't let a consultant undermine your self-confidence. Rely on your own judgment if the advice seems inappropriate. Be sure the fit is right for you! It isn't enough to make the consultant look good.*

30 *Simplicity*
20 Maxims on Quality

*T*he validity or usefulness of a management theory or system does not vary directly with its complexity.

All organizations are perfectly designed to get the results that they get.

Bigger isn't necessarily better; better is better.

Accountability pens people in and limits their activity; responsibility equal to authority challenges them and broadens their horizons.

The fact that the captain of the ship can clearly see the port is of no use if the crew continues to paddle in different directions.

The person into whose "In" basket you empty your "Out" basket is your customer.

A "problem" is the distance between where you are now and where you could be—no matter how good you are now.

Managers at all levels must return to their subordinates the authority they have slowly usurped over the years.

A pilot program is a last-ditch effort to avoid doing anything meaningful or difficult.

"Participative management" is an oxymoron; the phrase should be "participative leadership."

Responsibility for contributing to quality is a condition of employment—as natural as beginning work on time or attending a training class or picking up a paycheck.

Ironically, the customer group most often ignored is the one that is easiest to communicate with: fellow employees.

There are two common stumbling blocks to senior management commitment to a quality process: "This looks too easy" and "This looks too hard."

For an organization to judge a proposed quality process by its intricacy and high price is every bit as valid as a college professor grading term papers based on their weight and number of footnotes.

When every idea for improvement must go through a multilayer, "Mother-may-I?" approval procedure before implementation, small ideas will get lost.

American workers believe that "productivity" is a word meaning "They are coming after someone's job." They know for sure that "down-sizing" or "right-sizing" means "They are firing people."

Only take measurements that count.

Quality is an ordered, if not always orderly, business process.

"Trust is like a crystal bubble. Did you ever try to fix a crystal bubble?"   —*A third-grader*

"Two approaches to improvement to avoid: systems without passion and passion without systems."   —*Tom Peters*

Axiom #**30** *Simple can be profound. Sometimes a few words can get to the heart of the matter.*

31 *Trust*

An Old-Fashioned Story of Empowerment

*C*hip Bell is a management consultant and author based in Charlotte, North Carolina. He is also a marvelous story teller, a master at using an episode from his own experiences while growing up in southern Georgia to make a point about how individuals and organizations ought to conduct their business. Bell tells a story about Leroy Clark, the grocer in his hometown:[3]

> He was my introduction to the occupation labeled "merchant." Leroy was courteous, competent and eager to help all who came into his small, overstocked, all-purpose store. If you had told Leroy he was "customer-driven" he'd have looked at you funny, but that's what he was. Leroy knew a lot about service strategies and customer-friendly delivery systems and service recovery and front-line empowerment, though he was no scholar of service management.

On the topic of front-line empowerment, Bell tells this story about Leroy:

> I doubt the word "empowerment" ever passed Leroy's lips, but he empowered his only stock boy. Struggling one day to open a case of butter beans, the young man was embarrassed by a crude racial slur thrown at him by a couple of loud, white teenagers. Leroy calmly walked over to the rowdy boys and told them to get out. Before they were out of earshot, though, he turned to the stock boy and said, "Abel, I'm going to the bank. You know what to do, so you're in charge of the store while I'm gone."
>
> Now that sounds like small potatoes today, but in a very conservative Georgia country town in the early '50s, that was empowerment with a capital E. Leroy was not a saint, entirely untainted by the racial prejudice that pervaded his community. But he knew that if this young man were treated with respect, he would probably exhibit confidence and competence when serving the patrons of the

store. I wonder what Leroy would think today if he knew his leadership practices are frantically pursued by government commissions on "self-esteem" and by senior executives who are paid more in a year than Leroy earned in a lifetime?

It is as effective a story on the topic of trust and its public manifestation, empowerment, as you're likely to find.

Axiom #**31** *Trust is conveyed to employees in everyday behavior. It is not enough to say you trust someone; you have to demonstrate it.*

Part Two
On Participation

32 ab initio (from the beginning)

Framework for Participation

We are an intelligent species and the use of our intelligence quite properly gives us pleasure. In this respect the brain is like a muscle. When it is in use we feel very good.

Understanding is joyous.

> —*Carl Sagan*
> Broca's Brain *[1979], ch. 2*

Competition brings out the best in products and the worst in people. —*David Sarnoff [1891–1971]*

In order that people may be happy in their work, these three things are needed: They must be fit for it. They must not do too much of it. And they must have a sense of success in it. —*John Ruskin [1819–1900]*
> Pre-Raphaelitism *[1851]*

Axiom #32 *Participation presupposes that you are dealing with intelligent, cooperative, capable adults. If co-workers do not fit that description, participation presupposes that they can be encouraged to behave as if they do.*

33 Autonomy

In the Absence of Corporate Support, What One Employee Can Do

*T*he goal of every quality process is to increase customer satisfaction through improving the production processes for goods and services. Most discussion on quality processes takes place at the macro level: What can a company do to incorporate continuous improvement? Of equal interest, however, is the micro level: What can one employee do?

Everyone in an organization has internal customers, and everyone has a job description (whether formal or informal). Yet, rarely does one employee look at the requirements for her or his own job and then survey other employees to find out whether job specifications match other employees' expectations. Even an informal attempt to find out what internal customers really want is a step in the right direction.

As an example, consider Rose. Rose joined a financial services organization right out of high school; her good marks and typing skills helped her to win a job in a tight market and begin her life in the business world.

She learned the rudiments of her new position in the way so many new employees learn them—from the person she was replacing, who had been waiting for someone new to arrive so that she could move to a different department and a promotion. They had a three-hour "overlap."

At one point during the frenzied three hours (the first thing the outgoing "expert" had said was, "There's not much time, so just be quiet and listen"), the old hand said, "Oh, yeah, every Tuesday afternoon at 1:00, this box of cards is going to show up on your desk. Stop whatever you are doing and alphabetize them;

then put them on the desk behind you because Gloria works on them next. Once you get the hang of it, it'll take about an hour and ten minutes."

Rose quickly fell into the routine and performed well. She was obviously a hard worker, and her evaluations were all outstanding.

Every Tuesday afternoon at 1:00, her world stopped while she put the cards in alphabetical order. One week she did it in less than an hour.

Then came the fateful Tuesday just after she celebrated her second anniversary with the company. Rose had just put the box of freshly alphabetized cards on Gloria's desk and swung back around to her own desk when she remembered something she had meant to tell Gloria.

She turned back to Gloria, just in time to watch her dumping all the cards into her trash can. Rose reacted as virtually any mature business person would have reacted. "What are you doing?" she hollered.

"Oh," said a surprised Gloria, "I don't use these anymore— not since I started getting a printout about a year and a half ago."

Rose had not been deliberately wasting her time or the company's time and money for the last 18 months. She had been performing her tasks exactly as they had been explained to her. What she had not done was talk with her customer, Gloria, the person to whom she passed her work. She had never said to Gloria, "Hey, do you ever use these things?" much less, "Anything you'd rather see me do for you?"

Nor are such miscommunications confined to the lower echelons of the company. Here is a "quality exercise" for an executive: The next time you fill out that monthly report (you know the one, the one with all the required paragraphs, the one that requires you and your secretary to spend about three hours chasing down information), after you sign it, do not put it in the company mail system. Make up enough copies for everyone on the distribution list (usually on the left of the last page, just below your signature—you may need help to translate the code) and hand-deliver them. As you hand a copy to each person, ask him or her, "Do you read this? Which parts are useful? Anything else you'd like to see in this report?"

The most frequent answer is likely to be, "Well, I don't always actually read it, but we do file it."

The second most common response will probably be, "What report is this? Are you sure we get it?"

Third will be a variation of, "Oh, yeah, I use that number in paragraph 3B in my monthly report. Boy, am I glad you're always on time."

If you only cut the contents of your report by a third and your distribution list in half, it is well worth the effort.

What goes on inside an organization, out of view of the external, paying customers goes a long way toward defining what level of service the front-line employee will be able to provide. Poor work (including unnecessary work) ripples out to the external customer, either in the form of higher costs or a lack of time and information.

Axiom #33 *If the corporate philosophy does not change one iota, if there is no structure or training provided, here is one time-saving and money-saving step that anyone can take: Ask your internal customers what they want. A degree of autonomy is available to everyone.*

34 Balance
The Pros and Cons
of Employee Participation

*I*n a paper titled *Employee Participation and Involvement*, Professors David Levine and George Strauss of the University of California, Berkeley, included the following analysis of the theoretical benefits of employee participation:[1]

1. Participation may result in better decisions. Workers often have information which higher management lacks. Further, participation permits a variety of different views to be aired. *On the other hand*, workers may be less informed than managers and the premises upon which they make their decisions may be different. Further, if decisions are made by groups, reaction to changing environments may be particularly slow.

2. People are more likely to implement decisions they have made themselves. Not only do they know better what is expected of them, but helping make a decision commits one to it. *On the other hand*, once becoming committed to a decision, employees may be reluctant to change it.

3. The mere process of participation may satisfy such non-pecuniary needs as creativity, achievement, and social approval. *On the other hand*, not everyone has strong desires for creativity and achievement, or they satisfy these sufficiently off the job.

4. Participation may improve communications and cooperation; workers communicate with each other rather than requiring all communications to flow through management, thus saving management time. *On the other hand*, participation is time consuming.

5. Participative workers supervise themselves, thus reducing the need for full-time supervisors, and so reducing overhead labor costs.

6. Participation enhances people's sense of power and dignity. This reduces the need to show one's power through fighting management and restricting production. *On the other hand*, once a precedent of participation is established, withdrawal of the "right" to participate becomes difficult.

7. Participation increases loyalty and identification with the organization, especially if the group's suggestions are implemented. *On the other hand*, cohesive, participative groups may unite against management to restrict production and prevent change.

8. Participation frequently results in the setting of goals. There is considerable evidence that goal setting is an effective motivational technique.

9. Participation teaches workers new skills and helps train and identify leaders.

10. If participation takes place in a group setting, a new element is added: group pressure to conform to decisions adopted.

11. When union and management leaders jointly participate to solve problems on a non-adversarial basis, the improved rela-

tionship may spill over to improve union-management relations generally.

Obviously, participation is not without its disadvantages. In addition to those mentioned above, there are costs of retraining employees and managers and, perhaps, of redesigning technology. On balance, however, the advantages of participation outweigh the disadvantages for most workplaces. Thus, participation, if properly introduced, can be a powerful tool for increasing productivity.

Doctors Levine and Strauss concluded their paper with these "Policy Recommendations":

- The government should subsidize research, demonstration projects, and the dissemination of research concerning participation. This effort will lower the costs of introducing participation, and help the parties avoid the mistakes others have made.
- The administration should encourage the introduction of participation within the federal agencies [the paper predated the founding of the Federal Quality Institute]. Participation's potential advantages of committed workers, flexibility, higher quality, and so forth are valuable in the public sector as well as the private.
- The National Labor Relations Act should be revised to make it clear that participation programs are legal in both union and non-union settings, as long as their purpose is neither to bypass or avoid unions.
- Continuity of employment is an important condition for participation plans. Encouragement of participative plans is therefore one of the many benefits associated with full employment. Granting partial unemployment insurance for partial layoffs (i.e., job sharing), increasing the experience rating of unemployment insurance, and releasing Jobs Training Partnership Act funds for workers who have not yet been laid off, will reduce the indirect subsidy that firms that lay off workers receive from firms that strive to maintain full employment.
- Participation plans often take some initial investment in time and effort before improvements are seen. Any actions that the government could take to lengthen the time horizons of managers and investors would make it easier to invest in participation.
- More research is needed, especially to understand how to avoid the pitfalls which make so many programs fail.

Axiom #**34** *On balance, the known advantages of participation outweigh the known disadvantages.*

35 Canons
Four Canons of Participation

A canon is a basis for judgment, standard, or criterion. There are four participation canons by which a quality process can be assessed.

- **Canon #1.** *Everyone is enrolled.* This means that participation is nonvoluntary; anything less splits an organization into activists and bystanders. The nonvoluntary enrollment of every person on the payroll does not mean, however, that 100 percent of employees will be enthusiastic proponents of quality on the first day of the process. It does mean that a mechanism will be in place that allows every individual to take part in the continual improvement of the organization, even if someone does not "pitch in" until several months after the official beginning of the process.

- **Canon #2.** *Everyone has customers.* By defining "customer" as "anyone to whom you provide service, product, or information," the opportunity for every employee to be active in the process of continual improvement is strengthened.

- **Canon #3.** *Everyone has quality goals.* In a mature quality process, every individual on the payroll will have personal quality goals along with an understanding of how his or her individual goals support the accomplishment of unit and company objectives. These goals are developed through discussions between the individual, his or her peers, his or her customers, and, lastly, his or her work supervisor.

- **Canon #4.** *Implementation is bottom-up; commitment and support are top-down.* A quality process must be structured so that everyone can impact the system, not just so that the system can impact everyone.

Axiom *#***35** *Every human endeavor involving two or more people needs to be based on a common understanding of what rules apply.*

36 *Celebration*

Sometimes You've Just Got to Throw a Party

*C*elebrations are a part of human tradition. From dragging dinner into the cave by its tail to bringing home the district championship, achieving a goal has been a good enough excuse to throw a bash. The same principle applies in business, and it should not be limited to top executives sharing an expensive bottle of champagne to celebrate a big sale or a good year.

Celebrations of all kinds are appropriate: big and small, special occasions and annual events, public and private. Any corporate celebration usually has some brief "business" message, but keep in mind that it had better be brief and it had better fit in with the scheme of things. Use a light touch. Be a little corny. Brag, enjoy, have fun!

Quality is an ideal theme for a party. Pecten Chemicals Inc., Houston, Texas, had a guest speaker, announced their annual corporate goals, and conducted a sing-along. A group of employees led everyone through such potential standards as the "Pecten Team Song" and another ditty sung to the tune of the "Marine Corps Hymn":

FROM THE HALLS OF ONE SHELL PLAZA
TO THE SHORES OF JAPAN
WE'LL DELIVER OUR PRODUCTS
BY AIR OR SEA OR LAND
WE WILL MEET OUR CUSTOMER REQUIREMENTS
AND WILL DO IT RIGHT EACH TIME
WE ARE PROUD TO CLAIM THE TITLE
THE PECTEN QUALITY TEAM

Fluoroware, Inc., Chaska, Minnesota, held a special event to celebrate ZDDay (Zero Defect) and recognize employees for their efforts. It started with a boat ride across a little lake (little enough that it would have been just as easy to drive around). Each employee was given a cooler bearing the logo "Jazzed on Quality." Inside was a T-shirt, whistle, package of Life Savers (what else for a cruise?), bottle opener, and yo-yo; "Jazzed on Quality" was printed on every flat surface. Lunch, speeches, and recognition followed.

Then there was Carthage Machine Company in Carthage, New York. They launched their quality process with a community fête, featuring the junior high school band, town officials, retirees, and an enormous cake. McCormack and Dodge took a more low-profile approach in Natick, Massachusetts. On their launch date, executives of the company met employees at the door and gave them a set of three professionally designed posters celebrating their Quality Without Limits process.

Any organization with a well-prepared, structured quality process will find many occasions to celebrate. Paul Revere Insurance Group in Worcester, Massachusetts, involves their top few managers in recognizing team efforts throughout the year. They conducted over 1500 such recognition ceremonies during the first four-and-a-half years of the Quality Has Value process. Once a year, the entire company gathers in Mechanics Hall for an update on the Quality Has Value process and the presentation of awards to that year's Most Valuable Teams and Most Valuable Players. The company has shown videos of the top management team singing and dancing, presented slide shows featuring employees, distributed mugs, banners, balloons—anything to generate excitement. Once a year, the company also celebrates with a Qualifest, a fair giving teams a chance to brag about their accomplishments.

Nor does Paul Revere stop with routine events. In 1988, when the company was awaiting a visit from the Baldrige Award Examiners, the kitchen baked 1400 cookies in the shape of a "Q" to be given out by executives accompanying the morning snack cart route. Short-term programs, such as one that enabled employees to trade a thank-you note for a cactus with a "Stuck on Quality" sticker, pepper the process.

Celebrate often. Relying on one annual event is a mistake. If annual awards are presented in the context of a quality process where virtually everyone in the audience has been thanked by the organization one or more times during the course of the previous year, the audience's congratulations will be sincere. If no other awards or recognition are given out all year, it divides the company into two groups: those few who won and those many who tied for last place.

For any excuse or every excuse, celebration builds solidarity, loyalty, mutuality. By combining private one-on-one occasions with public galas, employees are assured that their efforts are appreciated—and that the entire company is involved in the continuous improvement of the organization.

Axiom #**36** *If a reason to celebrate arises, party. If it doesn't, look for a reason to celebrate.*

37 *Change*
Change Happens

Change Happens

*"Frankly, comrade, I think these changes are
coming too quickly . . ." —Jim Borgman*
Cincinnati Enquirer[2]

Axiom #**37** *Wouldn't it be better to be a part of deciding what
changes will be made rather than having to adjust to them?*

38 Communications

Improve Communications Skills: Check Reception—Listen Down

*T*he "corporate communications department" in many organizations is grossly misnamed. If truth were at a premium, it would be changed to the "corporate broadcast department," since almost all its activities are aimed at presenting messages. From personal presentations to videotapes to posters, and everything in between, specialists are on hand to turn a phrase or develop a visual. But broadcasting is only half of effective communications.

Equally important is "reception," which most organizations assume takes care of itself. On those occasions where there is a corporate attempt to ascertain how well a message has been conveyed, it is usually confined to messages relayed outside the company—for example, public relations and advertising. Rarely is any attempt made to gauge internal reception. One wag compared internal communications to tying a note on a rock labeled "do not return" and throwing it over a wall.

All management is responsible for internal reception, making it an infinitely complex problem. It behooves an executive who initiates a communication to find out whether what was heard is the same thing that he or she intended to convey. Conversely, when an executive receives a piece of information, it is the senior person's responsibility to ensure that she or he hears and understands what the person sending the message intended to say. This prevents a future exchange of, "But I told you," and "No, you didn't."

The odds of success are, of course, increased immeasurably if what is broadcast is clear and concise. Writing In *American Heritage,* Peter Baida lambasts executives who forget the basics: "I have received memos so swollen with managerial babble that they struck me as the literary equivalent of assault with a deadly weapon." This extends from routine memos to statements of quality "values" or "vision."

It also helps if the message is consistent. Ray Kroc, founder of McDonald's, noted, "If I had a brick for every time I've repeated the phrase 'Quality, Service, Cleanliness, and Value,' I think I'd probably be able to bridge the Atlantic Ocean with them." Such statements are of real value only if people are sure what is intended by them. If well understood and thoroughly—and repeatedly—disseminated, however, they can be the glue that binds a company together.

The only way to be certain that a communications effort is working is, of course, to talk to people—lots of people. Sentences that include phrases such as, "What I hear you saying is ..." or "Did I make myself clear? What did you hear?" need to be a frequent part of conversation with people deep within the organization. Do not take reception for granted; too much is at stake. Without effective communications to break down barriers, an organization quickly becomes a collection of semi-independent fiefdoms.

The most neglected aspect of corporate communications is "listening down." Few executives would maintain that they have nothing to learn from the people who buy their products and services. Yet these same executives act as if their employees have little of value to say. They treat internal communications solely as a way to make their views known, rarely actively soliciting opinions from those lower on the corporate ladder—unless they require a specific piece of information to make a specific decision.

The reason for this shortsighted behavior is an inability to acknowledge that, unlike corporate power, knowledge is not hierarchical. While it is proper to assume that your boss has the power to direct your subordinates to perform some task, knowledge does not work in the same neat way. If a person is at level "X + N" (your boss), it is not a valid assumption that he or she knows everything that is known by everybody at levels "X" and "X − N" (your level and below).

But if people believe that knowledge is hierarchical, it chokes off communication up the corporate ladder. If, for instance, someone sees a problem that is causing some loss in efficiency, he or she might think, "Well, I can see that there's a problem here . . . so my boss must see it too, since it is so obvious to me . . . but my boss doesn't direct it to be fixed . . . so my boss must know something else that I don't know that makes it necessary to do it this seemingly inefficient way . . . so I guess I'll just keep doing it this way as well as I can."

In truth, of course, the boss has not seen the particular inefficiency and, if alerted to it, would know of no reason to continue it.

The responsibility to break this pattern lies with the person at level "X + N." He or she must begin to ignore the years of training that has taught each member of the organization to "listen up" and "proclaim down." He or she must begin, instead, to "listen down," even to the extent of devising ways to tap into this largely hidden body of knowledge.

Listening down comes with assumptions and guidelines of its own:

- Not all wisdom is above you on the corporate ladder. Listening up only gives part of the picture.
- Listening down leads to decision making that is far better informed. There is no cause for shame in not knowing it all; there is a cause for shame in refusing to listen.
- Whether at the top of the organization or at the bottom, it is impossible to make intelligent decisions without accurate information. Withholding information is self-defeating.
- Successful listening includes taking action as a result of what is learned.
- Form can precede content. Formalized rules (e.g., a resolution to talk with three nonmanagement employees every Monday afternoon) are excellent ways to start new habits.

Axiom #**38** *Communications are vital to a successful quality process.*

39 Creativity

Wanted: Customer Service Employees Willing to Make an Extra Effort

*B*ecause so many employees of a service organization have personal contact with external (i.e., paying) customers, building and maintaining a high level of quality in a service organization is a complex challenge. On the other hand, precisely because there is that close connection, the potential for employees increasing customer satisfaction is enormous.

This puts an additional burden on service employees. They must not only adhere to the technical specifications for their job, but they must do it with the proper attitude. A line worker in a production facility who is in a bad mood but who has deeply ingrained habits of doing things carefully can still turn out products that are "fit for use." If, however, a waiter is in a bad mood and projects that mood to the customer, little else matters.

There is also a difference when it comes to recovery. A fast-thinking and sympathetic hotel clerk, for instance, can turn the discovery of a dead cockroach in the bed of a hotel room into a make-a-customer-for-life opportunity. On the other hand, no matter how careful (or cheerful) a member of an assembly line is, if someone else fails to do the job well, the product may be beyond salvaging.

A creative "fix" may be short term, but it can buy the service organization time to correct the process that caused the problem before another customer is affected. Professor Dick Chase of the University of Southern California Business School tells the following story:

> My wife and I were eating dinner in the basement of this college-crowd-oriented Mexican restaurant in Boston. While we were wait-

ing for our dinner to arrive, we observed a tiny mouse walking along the baseboard. The mouse would come out from behind some boxes of Corona beer, look around, and scamper back. This happened several times, and we and others watched with interest while the couple whose table was next to his pathway were munching their nachos, unaware of *el raton*. Coincidentally, the manager of the restaurant came to apologize for slow service, explaining that one of the ovens was down but hoped that a few beers on the house would help us pass the time. We, of course, appreciated the gesture and whispered conspiratorially that there was a mouse on the baseboard and we hoped that he could do something about it without disturbing the diners, who were unaware of the mouse's presence. His response was classic: "The mouse? Why that's Harry—he's been here for years. Everybody knows him. And you know what the good news is? There are no rats in our restaurant because mice and rats don't coexist!"

Chase's comment on the situation: "The service failure was a combination of slow service and the tangible evidence of vermin infestation. The manager handled both with aplomb, making us aware of his concern with our wait, and converting Harry from a health hazard to an amenity. (I never saw Harry on subsequent visits, but I asked after him.)"

The key to service quality is whether or not the employee feels committed enough to the organization to extend personal effort. If the employee feels as if he or she is a respected member of the organization, understands and buys into the corporate identity and goals, and is already involved in the continuous improvement of the company, the chances that he or she will bring that extra effort to bear substantially increase.

Axiom #39 *Service personnel are often the external customers' definition of quality. No matter what it says in the company service manuals, the customer only believes what he or she personally experiences. This puts an inordinate amount of pressure on the front-line employees of a service organization to be creative in meeting customer needs.*

40 *Effectiveness*
Little Things Mean a Lot

A fishing net with a very wide weave will catch only big fish. A net with a small, tight weave will catch the big fish—and it will also catch little fish. In any one haul from the sea, the total weight of the little fish will most likely outweigh the one or two big fish that have been caught.

Quality processes need to weave nets that can catch both big ideas and small ideas. Focusing only on the big ideas—the "breakthrough" ideas—handicaps the effectiveness of a quality process from the outset. Yet many programs established today overtly or covertly discourage small ideas in one of two ways:

- Companies insist that all ideas must be presented to management prior to implementation.

  Employees are well aware of the value of their top managers' time. Especially in those situations where a group knows that this is the only chance they will have to address top managers this month (or year), they will not "waste" time on ideas that "merely" reduce hassle or "only" save a few minutes or dollars.

- Companies provide incentives in the form of a percentage of savings.

  A common failing of suggestion box systems, this reduces the exchange to one of an employee "selling" his or her idea to the management. It also virtually insures that there will not be any small ideas at the monthly (or quarterly) meetings of the suggestion system committee.

The Japanese even have a word for the philosophy of incremental improvement: *kaizen*. While they do not discount progress from major innovations, they believe that companies that encourage small ideas benefit greatly. Toyota, for instance, has built its suggestion system up over the last two decades to the point that it now regularly receives over 2.6 million ideas annually from its employees. That is an average of over 60 ideas per employee per year (for each of which there is the same token monetary recognition). One reason for this astounding rate of involvement is that 95 percent of the ideas are implemented!

Very few of those 2.6 million ideas are big ideas with sweeping ramifications. Many are, in fact, quite limited in their impact. If, however, one were to multiply "2.6 million" times "quite small," the product is "huge."

Companies that encourage small ideas are playing the odds. It is far easier to find 100 people who can each improve things by 1 percent than it is to find one magician who can single-handedly improve things by 100 percent. Magicians are great; reliance on magicians is not. If one of 100 employees has a bad day, there is still a chance at a 99 percent improvement. If one magician has a bad day . . .

Axiom #**40** *If the quality movement in America ever gets organized to the point of choosing a theme song, it should be "Little Things Mean a Lot." It is the continual flow of small ideas that is the heart and soul of quality improvement. Being alert to every opportunity also makes it more likely that the big ideas will surface.*

41 Empowerment
A Tale of Puzzled Participation

*T*he boss was a self-proclaimed disciple of the Ancient consultant, Mough (see *An Ancient Fable*, page 1). He liked measurements. When he first discovered the writings of Mough, he applied the lessons therein to his company, and there had been an immediate beneficial impact on the bottom line. Money was saved; productivity increased.

Progress, however, leveled off after a couple of years, and no amount of new measurements seemed to help. In fact, there were even some employees who balked at taking more measurements.

Then the boss began hearing about something called "empowerment." "Empowered Employees" were said to be the key to the future.

That sounded good. So the boss looked at his measurements and began picking his best employees. When all the employee evaluation measurements agreed that a particular employee was one of the best, the boss would send for that employee to come to his office.

The employee would stand in front of the boss's desk and the boss would say, "You are a good employee. The measurements prove that. You've gotten great numbers. So I am hereby making you an Empowered Employee."

Frequently, the employee was so overcome by the emotion of the moment that tears of happiness flowed forth.

One day, George was invited to the boss's office. "George," the boss said, "you are one of our best. You have great numbers. The measurements all point to you as one of the best. Therefore I am making you an Empowered Employee."

George began to smile, but suddenly he stopped and asked, "I want to thank you for the honor, sir, but what does it mean?"

"What does it mean?" repeated the boss. "What do you mean, 'What does it mean?' It means you are empowered." The boss was flustered. Nobody had ever asked before.

"Well," continued George, "I really don't want to appear ungrateful because I am very flattered and pleased, but what does it mean to be empowered? How have things changed? Do I measure it, too? What can—and should—I do now that I wasn't already doing before I was empowered?" George was both sincere and embarrassed; the boss could see that.

The boss was a fair man. He said, "Can I get back to you on that? How about this time next week?"

"Thanks," said George. "I really didn't mean to cause any trouble. But if you want me here, I'll be here next week. Thank you again."

The boss called in the head of Measurement, Research & Development and repeated George's question. "I'm not sure," said the head of MR&D. "I know I've seen it in the title of several books and articles lately."

"I told him I'd have an answer in a week," said the boss. "Why not start by seeing what the other Empowered Employees are doing?"

"Good idea," said the head of MR&D. "I'll have them surveyed immediately."

Two days later, the head of MR&D reported back. "All of the EE's (technical survey-talk for Empowered Employees) report being very happy with their designation. They report that it really makes them 'feel good' to be empowered—and they really appreciated the time you took with them."

"Yes," said the boss, "but what does it mean? What are they doing differently?"

"Apparently nothing," said the head of MR&D. "A few commented that they had thought of doing something but weren't sure what their bounds were so they hadn't done it. Oh, yes, they also said that employees of other companies were jealous that they had been empowered. It appears to be a real status thing to be an EE."

"But what does it mean? Haven't we measured the impact of empowering our employees?"

"I'm afraid not. Back when you started this program, I did talk with a counterpart of mine in another company here in town who said that the empowerment of employees wasn't something that a specific measure could be applied to, that it was bigger than that. Since we already had plenty to do, we never tried to pin it down further."

"Are you still friends with that person?" asked the boss. "Could you ask him to come over here for a conversation?"

"The person is a 'she,' and she is standing outside the office right now," the head of MR&D replied, pleased that he had correctly anticipated the boss's request.

"Please invite her in."

The boss and the friend of the head of MR&D talked for several hours that day and the next. The boss was astounded to learn that Mough's Ancient guidance was only part of the total picture. He had never heard of Lawrence and Curleigh.

When the week was up, George appeared at the boss's office right on time. The boss asked him to come in and sit down.

"I've done a lot of thinking and talking in the past week, George," the boss said. "I want to thank you for asking that question last week. I don't have the complete answer for you yet, but I'm working on understanding the answer and so is my staff. I can, however, give you a partial answer that will enable you to get started."

"I'd like that," said George. "I really didn't mean to cause a fuss. I've always enjoyed working here."

"The beginning place for an answer to your question is 'authority equal to responsibility,'" the boss said. "I suspect it will also be the ending place, but we've got a lot of learning to do before we fully understand it. A new friend of mine says that 'authority equal to responsibility' is 'empowerment with defined bounds—defined bounds give a person freedom to act.' That makes sense to me, George. How's it sound to you?"

"Well, if I hear you right, 'authority equal to responsibility' sounds a bit like I am empowered to change those things that I am responsible for. Is that close?"

"That's great, George. My new friend puts it more bluntly. She says, 'If their butt is on the line for it, they get to change it— and their boss realizes that it is not fair to blame someone who is only doing what they've been told to do and have no power to change.' We are going to incorporate this philosophy into the entire organization in the coming months, so I'm afraid that being an empowered employee won't be so special anymore."

"You think not?" asked George.

Axiom #**41** *Even a sound management practice can be reduced to the status of a fad if words are used without understanding. In the case of empowerment, everyone must not only be alert to possibilities for change, but they must also be able to make changes when appropriate. Only then will quality improve continuously.*

42 *Follow-Up*

Suggestion? What Suggestion? (When Quality Ideas Go Astray)

A medical technologist at a small community hospital in central Massachusetts has been doing battle with her organization's suggestion box system for over two years. Her unflagging attempts to offer ideas for improvement have met with little success; instead she has uncovered a labyrinth of unpublished rules, hidden agendas, and indifference.

On the first occasion, she submitted a suggestion concerning an appropriate recognition of senior employees' work anniversaries. Not wishing to appear overzealous, she waited a year before asking the head of the suggestion box committee what had become of her suggestion. "Oh, we don't convene a meeting until we have six suggestions," she was told.

After resubmitting her suggestion, she discovered that the hospital regulations already allowed for a more generous recognition of the work anniversary than she had suggested. That was the good news. The bad news was that her immediate superior asked her to keep her newly acquired knowledge secret.

The following year, she dropped another completed form in the box. Specifically, she suggested it might be a good idea to list the types of insurance that the hospital accepted in the next advertisement that they ran in the local paper. Eight months later, at the beginning of the hospital's next ad campaign, there was a list of accepted insurance companies as part of the copy.

She had not heard from the suggestion box committee.

A quick investigation revealed that when the secretary of the executive who was the head of the suggestion box committee read the suggestion, she thought it was such a good idea, she forwarded it directly to the Public Relations Department. Meanwhile, the committee had never heard of it.

When last contacted, the medical technologist had once again submitted an idea. Two weeks later when she looked inside the box, her idea was still there. "It isn't a suggestion box," she summarized. "It's a dead letter box."

Axiom *#***42** *No system is inherently failure proof or failure prone. A lot depends on the company's follow-up procedures and how well they are executed. Dr. W. Edwards Deming states flatly that at least 85 percent of all quality problems can be laid at the door of management. In some companies, the percentage is higher.*

43 Fun
Seriously, Organize Some Fun

As with the concept of quality as a whole, the idea of insuring that a workplace is a setting for, and a source of, enjoyment has a very practical aspect. Individuals who find their workplace pleasurable do their jobs better. When people get satisfaction from their accomplishments, appreciate the inevitable humor in their surroundings, and have an honest appreciation for the relative importance of their various tasks, they work more efficiently and more effectively.

Seriousness and fun are not, after all, mutually exclusive. In fact, they are complementary—witness the fame of the cartoon strip *Doonesbury*. Without a sense of humor and a sense of proportion, there are no gradations of seriousness. Everything becomes an equally tense-jawed crisis. And when a *real* emergency develops, the story of the boy crying "Wolf!" is replayed.

These two qualities—a sense of humor and a sense of proportion—are so precious that they should be nurtured carefully when discovered in a subordinate and appreciated deeply when evinced by a superior. It is possible to discriminate between genuine humor and mere giddiness or between balanced judgment and a refusal to take anything seriously. Encourage the former, discourage the latter.

There is even a growing body of evidence that laughter is physically beneficial, that a good laugh decreases heart rate, lowers blood pressure, increases blood flow to the brain, and releases endorphins—the same biochemical painkillers widely credited with producing the "runner's high."

Happily, the increasing awareness of the positive impact of making humor a natural component of the work environment is being translated into action. Companies have begun to hire "elation strategists" or establish "Fun Committees" who have, as a primary or collateral duty, the responsibility to help employees see the lighter side of their work day.

Writing in *Psychology Today*, David J. Abramis offered the following guidelines on making work more playful:[3]

Make a conscious effort to have fun. Set fun goals for yourself and your subordinates—such as attending the company get-togethers more regularly and setting up challenges for yourself—just as you set more traditional goals of performance and accomplishment.

You might even include "having fun" as a goal when you set performance objectives.

Spread the word. Let people know that having fun at work is appropriate—this might not have been true in their previous job. Share your information on how fun can be productive as well as pleasant and emphasize that both the individual and the organization play a part in making work fun.

Help supervisors and other managers have fun and suggest ways they can help their people do the same. Their influence is crucial, for good or bad. When we asked, "What would make your job more fun?" a number of people told us, "Get rid of my supervisor."

At the other extreme, a salesman explained how his boss "set up a whole day of fun and play through a Sales Olympics. It's a big sports and games day in which sales teams compete against each other." Another supervisor "tries to open every weekly meeting with a joke." In a manufacturing firm, one man told us, "Our managers constantly joke with each other. It sure reduces the tension of 60-hour weeks."

Ask people what they think is fun. Because this varies so much, you need to fit the fun to each person and each situation.

Use rewards and recognition to let people know they are valued. Organizations such as Detroit-based Domino's Pizza, North American Tool & Die, a San Leandro, California, producer of metal stamping, and others ... recognize achievement with parties, awards, celebrations and plenty of public pats on the back. Every manager and supervisor should be expected to recognize successes and accomplishments, large or small. The rewards don't have to be formal or bureaucratic; they can be spontaneous and personal, appropriate to the circumstances.

Create events. Devise or increase the number of planned activities, such as contests, company-sponsored parties and sports, that add to fun in work. They all may help. But the biggest benefit is likely to come from creating fun in the work itself, in groups and social interactions and in relations with superiors.

Hire people who are interested in and capable of having fun. At Dreyer's Grand Ice Cream, for example, people aren't made supervisors unless they have the ability to create fun and arouse enthusiasm in others. It may be easier to hire this ability than to train a grim M.B.A. to laugh.

The organizations that are moving ahead of the pack these days invariably talk about their "culture" and being a "family." Only families whose members enjoy being around each other stay together for long.

Axiom #**43** *"Whistle while you work."—The Seven Dwarfs*
Alternate Axiom #43 "Be happy at your work."—Mao Tse Tung

44 *Individualism*

Collective Action Can Also Work for Individualists

Japan gets the most out of ordinary people by organizing them to adapt and succeed. America, by getting out of their way so that they can adjust individually, allows them to succeed.   *—James Fallow*
                                        The Atlantic Monthly

Americans have always been a contrary bunch; their heroes have long been the "cowboys" who bucked society, who carved out their own path. As a result, when the impact of "Japanese quality products" hit the American marketplace in the 1970s and 1980s, suggesting superiority of the more uniform Japanese approach to work, something very near panic ensued. Were the American workers going to have to give up their rugged individualism in order to succeed in the new economic order?

Actually, the choice is not between individual action and collective action, although early "experts" in the field of quality alienated many American business people—management and nonmanagement alike—by framing out the debate that way. The best choice is to devise a means of collective action that gives free rein to individual talents. Properly led, Americans can and do act in concert in their own best interests. They will, however, insist on having their individual judgments taken seriously and being given independence of action whenever possible. And it has been that way in America for a long time.

An instructive case in point occurred over two hundred years ago. Prior to the arrival of Baron von Steuben at Valley Forge in the winter of 1777, the American army had been generally ineffective. Consisting primarily of men on one-year contracts, it was capable of the occasional brilliant moment, but long-term success seemed far out of reach. The men were willing to do their time, but that was about it.

The addition of a Prussian general (especially one with credentials as suspect as von Steuben's) hardly seemed like the best move. The Prussians were well known, after all, for their top-down autocratic style of leadership. Fortunately, von Steuben was no ordinary Prussian.

His genius—and his success—came in his recognition that this American soldier he was now dealing with was a very different breed than his European counterpart. While the European soldiers had long been trained to move and fight as a single unit without asking any questions, the Americans wanted to know "why." So von Steuben told them, in great and repetitious detail. And he listened to them as well.

These Americans wanted to be trained before they were set to a task. So von Steuben trained them, mixing in a sense of humor only heightened by his fractured English.

The open communications did not mean that the soldiers were not expected to go through exhaustive drills and, in fact, to risk their lives if necessary. It did mean that they were treated as part of the solution, as thinking human beings who could contribute and who should be listened to.

After the winter in Valley Forge, the von Steuben-trained army of the American Revolution was never again defeated.

There are many examples of group activity in American culture—from wagon trains to quilting bees and barn raisings, from political parties to labor unions and P.T.A.'s. In many respects, it is easier and more natural for an individualist to judge when and how his or her action can contribute to a team effort than it is for someone whose identity depends on a team to begin to act independently. American individualism is an advantage.

Axiom $^{\#}\mathbf{44}$ *When participation makes each individual's unique contribution work for the organization, it taps into one of America's strengths.*

45 *Initiative*
On Banks, Planes, Pizzas, and Post Offices. . . A Service Potpourri

*I*n Sweden, a gentleman entered a large and very crowded bank to conduct some routine business. He was obviously shaking and seemed perplexed at seeing the long line. After attracting the attention of a teller, he asked, "I wonder if you can help me. I have not been well recently and am on medication that often makes me dizzy. I have no objection to waiting my turn, but I am afraid that if I try to stand in line, I may faint. Would it be possible to get a chair for me and somehow mark my place in line so that I can be waited on in turn?"

The teller looked at the line and at the gentleman and said that tellers always served the next person in line; no one had ever requested special treatment before. Would he please join the line and give it a try? His wait would only be a minute or so.

Twenty minutes later, he began to feel genuinely ill and again proposed that he be seated while he waited his turn. "I really don't mind waiting, but I am increasingly dizzy," he told the teller. He was assured that the line was moving rapidly; if he would just take his place, it would be his turn shortly.

He got back in line.

When he came to, he was surrounded by anxious-looking bank employees. A quick conference resulted in the decision that an exception could be made. Since there was now no doubt that the man truly could not wait in line, employees showed him to a separate room and asked him to have a seat there.

And promptly forgot him.

—From the files of the
Service Research Center of the
University of Karlstad, Sweden

The young man behind the USAir counter was brisk but friendly. Considering that the couple was checking in 11 pieces of luggage, it was an attractive combination. The airport was small, and a crowd was growing to meet the incoming flight. Voices inquired about the flight status—was it on time? late? what gate?

Excusing himself momentarily, the young man checked the flight board to see what gate information was posted and then picked up a phone to see if the flight had landed. "Flight 340 is in at gate 2," he announced to the crowd in general and then pulled two display numbers out from under the counter. On the front was the official lettering, and on the back were the two letters "I" and "N." Noting the couple's interest, he began to explain. "We're too small for an electronic board, and the airline doesn't supply anything to put on the manual board to let people know what's going on. So, I used "White Out" to paint "IN" on the back of these, and I post them as soon as I know the plane is here. It doesn't stop all the questions, but it helps. It keeps the baggage check line shorter since I don't have to stop as often."

The crowd dispersed, others stopped to read the board, baggage tags were stapled to tickets, and wishes for a pleasant flight extended. "Where would I go to meet Flight 340," a harried voice broke in. "Flight 340 is just in at gate 2 to your left," a pleasant smile for the questioner and the couple, and the young man turned back to the line. "Next, please."

—*Worcester, Massachusetts*

A letter contained the following tale:

> I decided to have a pizza delivered. An outfit called Blackjack Pizza (I don't know how widespread they are) continually sticks coupons in my door, so I decided to give them a try. The coupon listed two locations, both near me. I checked a map, picked the one that looked closer, called and ordered.
>
> Twenty minutes later, the telephone rang. Naturally, I expected it to be the driver calling to ask directions. Instead, it was the store calling to say that I was out of their area and to give me the number of their other store, whose area I was in.
>
> The immediate questions, of course, are:
>
> 1) Why did it take 20 minutes (a time in which Domino's would have had a pizza at my door) for them to tell me they couldn't deliver to me?
>
> 2) Once they decided that, why didn't they call and place the order with the other store? Aren't they related?
>
> As I said, I don't know how widespread this outfit is, but I doubt that it will grow very much. I threw away the coupon, made some sort of dinner at home, and decided not to order from them again. I wish I had had the presence of mind to ask the questions of the employee, but even if I had, it sounded like a kid who was in command of little else but the order desk, if that.
>
> —*Paul, an observer of life*

A subsequent postcard brought the news that Blackjack Pizza was no longer in business at that location.

The Orlyonok Hotel near the Lenin Central Stadium is not noted for dealing with Westerners, but the post office off the lobby is prepared. The elderly woman behind the counter has worked out a system guaranteed to expedite transactions in any language. Under one portion of the clear counter cover are samples of the postcards available. Under another, the numbers 1 to 31 are clearly displayed. By pointing first to one and then to another, it is possible to get any number of any postcard (when available). The amount owed is then calculated on an abacus and indicated using the numbers and a smile.

Watching a gaggle of different nationalities complete their business, one observer was moved to try to communicate how clever the system was. Not a word was exchanged, but the meaning was. Indicating the counter display, the foreigner applauded softly. Tapping the side of her head, the woman behind the counter assumed a shrewd expression and winked.

—Moscow, Russia

Axiom [#]**45** *Employees who feel capable of solving problems, do. This activity often takes place in spite of, not because of, corporate policies. Lack of initiative is often directly related to rules and regulations that limit alternatives or to inadequate training—both of which are beyond employee control.*

46 Issues
Corporate Roadblocks to Achieving Quality

*T*he training department of a major service organization polled students in 44 classes held in preparation for the company's imminent quality process. The goal was to find out what the students anticipated would be "roadblocks" to establishing an effective quality process in their organization. Five points were mentioned by 75 percent to 90 percent of the respondents:

Lack of Resources/Unrealistic Schedules
Unrealistic commitments; antiquated or outdated systems; lack of people; intervals not sufficient; everything due yesterday; unrealistic

demands by users; rigid due dates; better people get all work and other people slide; staffing freeze; mandated schedules; not enough terminals to access data bases; insufficient time to meet new product introduction guidelines

Lack of Communications

Departmental; interdepartmental; management structure hinders communications; don't get whole picture of what we want to accomplish (filtered); lack of honest communication, e.g.,—no raise for us, but execs received a raise; insufficient details at all levels; not enough access to top levels; too many people in process; too often focus on dotting i and crossing t—not on the intent of memo; miscommunications; assumptions amongst ourselves

Lack of Training

Internal as well as our customers; lack of knowledge/experience; lack of cross-training; can't keep up with technology; supervisor unwilling to make employee available; insufficient training when moved to new job; not trained in time; skills lost when training not put to use; don't train employees or customers on new products; what's available?

Lack of Teamwork/Cooperation

Responsibility—credit for you, blame for me; finger-pointing (in lieu of solution finding); not wanting to accept responsibility—it's not my job; look out for #1, not team; lack of vacation coverage—nobody picks up work; cooperation went out with reorganization; people don't share info; competition amongst departments (and people); lack of team effort (even within a geographical locale); poor coordination among groups; absurd departmental parochialism; too much putting monkey on someone else's back; no sharing of knowledge (not helping others coming for help); teamwork not focused on

Lack of Definition

Unclear specs/requirements; "by the time it gets down to my level, the definition is lacking"; no time to define requirements; no written commitments (service agreements) from major internal customers; changing requirements; incomplete definitions

In addition, from 45 percent to 75 percent of the respondents/ students also mentioned roadblocks in these categories: politics, conflicting priorities, poor planning/direction, and leadership/direction/decision making.

Finally, these categories were mentioned by less than 45 percent: lack of understanding of definition of job processes, employee morale, paperwork/red tape, resistance to change, lack of standard language, working environment, lack of recognition, reorganization/constant change, and use of consultants.

It is regrettable but not surprising that the company subsequently suffered through a long strike. Several years later, it is still hoping to initiate its quality process.

Axiom #**46** *Employees are well aware when management abdicates responsibility. Allocation of resources, communications, training, teamwork/cooperation, and definition of specifications are all management issues. Unless management is willing to solve these problems, it cannot expect employees to solve problems in their own work areas.*

47 *Mastery*
On-the-Job Training Is a Lousy Way to Learn

Remember the childhood game in which one person whispers a story to another, then that person tries to retell the story as accurately as possible to another, and on down the chain of living, breathing, receiver/transmitters? The fun of the game came in hearing the last person in the chain recount out loud what they had been told.

The grown-up version of that same game is called on-the-job training (or OJT). It is every bit as accurate as the childhood game. As each person trains the next, they—intentionally or not—introduce their own prejudices and preferences for how to do a particular task. Rather than returning continuously to a defined standard, task performance drifts further and further from either doing the right thing or doing things right.

Many employees have been forced to resort to OJT by their penny-wise management who in times of revenue shortfall frequently move unwittingly to prolong the company's problems by cutting back on training. This inevitably results in a declining standard for products and services.

Companies that excel, that dominate their market niches, have a common orientation toward training: the realization that training is not an expense but an investment. Management guru Tom Peters's advice is simple: "If your company is doing well, double your training budget; if your company is not doing well, quadruple it."

In addition to the impact on performance, training programs have a disproportionate impact on motivation. A new employee who is immediately scheduled for a company orientation class followed by a series of job-specific training courses knows that he or she is viewed as a valuable resource by the company. The alternative is grim. Being thrown into the pool to learn how to swim doesn't work with small children, and it doesn't work with new employees. The survivors of either carry a grudge for a long, long time.

Axiom #**47** *Continuous learning, returning to the classroom for formal instruction, as well as undergoing formalized mentor relationships, is needed to master the skills necessary to stay abreast of accelerating change. Companies that include quality-related subjects in their curriculum, in addition to traditional job skills, are better prepared to meet the future.*

48 Memory
What Happens When the Corporate Memory Retires?

A large manufacturing firm in southern Connecticut decided to subcontract an item that they had been casting in-house. Along with the contract specifications and directions, they gave their new subcontractor the mold that they had been using successfully for years.

For the first 36 months, not a single one of the subcontracted items was rejected. Every piece fit precisely where it was supposed to, just as it had when the company itself was making the part.

Then, one day, the rejection rate jumped from 0 percent to 100 percent.

The results of such an aberration were predictable. Without the subcontracted component, production of the larger assembly ground to a halt amid a flurry of finger-pointing. The subcontractor swore that they had done nothing different on their end; they were still using the original mold and following all the procedures they had followed for years. The manufacturer was equally certain that nothing had changed on their end.

The manufacturer was wrong. It turned out that Fred had retired.

Fred had been the first person to handle that particular piece. He had *always* been the first person. No matter who made the part, it was his work station that received the item from the mold.

Back when the piece had first been designed and the mold had first been made, Fred had noticed a burr on the surface of the piece. Fred figured it probably came from a small fault in the mold and filed the burr off. He also took action to try to correct the defect. He mentioned the problem and his opinion as to its source to his superiors. He mentioned it several times.

Nothing happened, so he took to carrying a file in his pocket. Each time he picked up a new part, the first thing Fred did was file off the little burr. After a while it got to be automatic for him, and he stopped mentioning it to anyone.

And then he retired.

Axiom #**48** *Lower-ranking employees are the corporate memory. They know more about the production of products and services, and the processes that are used, than they (or anyone else in the organization) are aware of. Even when they are ignored, these men and women continue to do their best—and their best becomes so routine that they fail to realize how special their knowledge and their contributions are.*

49 Negotiation
On Dealing with the Quality Purists

*C*ompanies thank employees for their efforts for the same reason that Goldilocks thanks the Three Bears on page 137: First, they deserve it, and second, it encourages them to repeat desired activities. Every quality process, however, will be faced with a few "purists" who will dispute the first, doubt the efficacy of the second, and take it upon themselves to guard the sanctity of the entire operation.

These purists often appear just before recognition is about to be extended to a successful employee or team of employees. "But wait," they say to the person responsible for the administration of the process, "there's no reason to reward anyone for doing *that*.

It's part of the job description; they should have been doing it all along."

While this might be true, it is also irrelevant. And it is best dealt with in the following manner: "Okay, assuming that this is included in the job description, were employees doing it before? Are they doing it now? Did the quality process act as a catalyst, a means for getting from where they were to where they are now? Good, then we'll say thank you."

Just because some task is included in a dust-gathering job description does not mean that it is integrated into the day-to-day performance of the job. When an employee receives his or her paycheck for months despite having not performed the particular task under discussion, there is de facto proof the company does not consider the task to be on the "things I should really do" list. Once a person (or team) decides to execute *any improvement*, whether in the job description or not, recognition serves to mark the occasion and to redefine the employee's understanding of the "real" job.

Purists also have difficulty distinguishing between an incentive and a thank you. They are right when they argue the case against incentives; incentives quickly degenerate into entitlements. What purists fail to realize, however, is that while you cannot compel sustained effort with incentives, employees who feel that their company genuinely values their efforts are likely to continue to look for ways to improve quality.

Distinguishing between a thank you and an incentive is easy in a social setting. You don't precipitate an invitation to dinner with a bottle of wine or a bouquet of flowers for your host or hostess, but you do increase your chances of being asked back by saying thank you with the same items. Timing is part of the difference. A thank you is after the fact. There is also a mutual understanding of what the interaction means. When companies reward behavior they wish to have repeated, they have to be sure that everyone knows they are saying "thank you" and not wistfully indulging in bribes.

The participation purist is also sensitive to the motives that employees espouse for improving quality. Only the most altruistic motives pass their scrutiny. This is usually expressed in an antipathy to including material items (to include cash or spendable certificates) in any plan for recognition, gratitude, and celebration. "You shouldn't do it," they say. "If you reward people with something with a monetary value for making improvements, employees will start doing things for the wrong reason."

It is an interesting academic argument. From a hardheaded business viewpoint, the important thing is not why employees improve quality but that they do improve it. Whether the employee was motivated by a thank you in the form of a clock radio or by an esoteric loyalty for the firm or a deep personal admiration for the CEO, who cares? The improvement is the same. Ideally, of course, quality itself is the ultimate motivator.

For some people a gift with tangible worth—no matter how small—connotes appreciation. For others, personal recognition of some kind is more potent. It is precisely because different people respond to different types of motivation that an organization bent on establishing a formal quality process must include a varied program of recognition.

Axiom #**49** *The quality purists are valuable in that they force conscious thought to justify steps sometimes taken instinctively. Surprised at the axiom? Don't be. Part of improving quality is understanding why something works or fails to work. There will be lots of uncomfortable questions. Only when answers have been negotiated can you proceed with confidence.*

50 *Personalities*

Great Minds Do (Not) Think Alike

*T*he meeting is over. You step into the hall furious because the entire afternoon was wasted. All that talk and no decision! Your co-worker approaches. "Don't you think we're moving too fast on the Ross project? We hardly have any facts, and already we're being pushed to make up our minds." Same meeting. Different minds.

The first step in conflict resolution is a respect for individual personalities. People are interested in different things; they get their information in different ways; they process information in different ways; they reach conclusions in different ways. *Please Understand Me*, a book by David Keirsey and Marilyn Bates, sets up four dichotomies for understanding why people respond differently to the same situation:

- Extroverting or Introverting: Where do you focus attention? How do you get energized?
- Sensing or Intuiting: How do you find out about things? How do you perceive your world?
- Thinking or Feeling: How do you interpret what you find out? How do you make decisions?
- Judging or Perceiving: How do you create your work and life style?

Group dynamics depend in large part on how individuals in the group answer these questions. Do you know what your own bias is? Do you know what the implications are?

The Keirsey and Bates book was written to help laymen. It makes no pretense to research or counseling purposes, but it is

123

invaluable for helping individuals recognize how they interact with others—and why they are uncomfortable with someone else's behavior.

Axiom #**50** *Teams begin with individuals. Respect for the different ways that different people process information is an excellent first step toward helping diverse personalities reach consensus.*

51 *Perspective #1*
An Abridged History of Participation in Three Questions

"**W**ho can we make accountable for this quality stuff?"

This question from top management marked the beginning of the first formal efforts at quality in America. The response was Quality Control specialists trained in measurement and stationed next to the door to the loading dock with instructions to "Stop the bad stuff." Everyone else's job remained the same: make quota—even if it meant slipping bad stuff past the Quality Control folks. At the end of the month if the shipping quota remained unfilled, Quality Control people could be sent off to a seminar. With Horatio no longer there to guard the bridge, quota could be met.

The best comment on this approach to quality is credited to that great American philosopher Lily Tomlin, who once mused, "Quality. If it's so good, why do we keep trying to control it?"

"Who can we get to volunteer to take care of this quality stuff?"

As markets toughened in the late 1970s and consumers started complaining or, worse yet, shopping elsewhere, top management asked employees to volunteer for Quality Circles. About 10 percent did; about 90 percent did not. In most cases, Quality Circles were assigned problems, asked to find solutions, and required to make presentations to management—who would then give or withhold permission to institute changes. Still, this made executives and consultants happy; it gave them an opportunity to look serious about involving employees in the effort to improve quality without having to delegate authority.

Not surprisingly, big problems were assigned, virtually to the exclusion of little problems. Even worse, in most companies only nonmanagement personnel were allowed on circles, suggesting one of two things: Either management never made mistakes (after all, only nonmanagement personnel were asked to improve) or members of management were so dimwitted that they couldn't improve even if given an organized chance.

"Who should we exclude from this quality stuff?"

Unlike the first two approaches in which top management determined a subset of the payroll to make responsible for quality, this question tries to identify the opposite subset, "Whose efforts can we afford to ignore?" Put another way, is there anyone to whom the CEO would be willing to say, "Fred [or Freida], we've had a meeting of top management, and we've decided that you are as dumb as old dirt and most likely will never have an original thought the rest of your life. So we're excluding you from our quality process"? If not, everybody is responsible for improving quality.

The mechanics of 100 percent participation can vary from suggestion systems to self-managing teams. The best approaches have two characteristics: They match authority with responsibility, creating a high degree of autonomy, and they capture both small and large ideas.

Axiom #**51** *Be sure you are using the right perspective when you set your goal. Is the goal to inspect in quality, to tackle large problems, or to improve quality overall? Only 100 percent participation can achieve the latter.*

52 Perspective #2
An Abridged History of Quality

*S*wedish researcher, writer, and consultant on service quality, Evert Gummesson believes that quality has matured to different degrees in the various segments of the economy.[4] Using the analogy of a lifetime of quality, his assessment of the development of quality is broken down into four stages.

Product Quality: The Grand Old Man began with systematic quality efforts in manufacturing in the 1920s. While often misused when applied to services, product quality can contribute to service quality for two reasons: 1) Service operations need products (consumables, capital goods), and 2) its long tradition has developed powerful tools that may be adjusted to services.

Since the 1970s, **Service Quality: The Adolescent** has developed new approaches based on the unique features of service. Although service quality has been heavily criticized and still has a long way to go, there has been strong interest among researchers and practitioners.

Even newer is **Computer Software Quality: The Juvenile Delinquent**. While crucial for service organizations, quality control in this area is not mature due to unique quality problems that need unique quality management methods.

Gummesson proposes a **Holistic Quality: The Baby** which will integrate thinking from all the quality areas. His view is that holistic quality will recognize several key factors:

- That all organizations produce and sell both goods and services but in varying proportions, and that the customer is buying utility and need satisfaction, not products or services as such (there are exceptions: certain products or services have a symbolic or personal value in themselves);

- That quality, productivity, and profitability are interconnected;
- That service operations are heavily dependent upon information technology and thus software quality is crucial for service quality;
- That the three types of quality are different in nature and have unique features that must be considered;
- The need to approach quality also from a deeper, humanistic perspective with the L-factor, "love" in its widest sense, as the key.

While he views holistic quality as a baby, Gummesson concludes, "Great hopes attached to him when he grows up; may he assume leadership in the quality battle-field."

—Research Report
Service Quality: A Holistic View
Evert Gummesson
Service Research Center of the
University of Karlstad, Sweden

Axiom #**52** *There is heavy debate in the field of quality over the relative merits of manufacturing versus service quality. Keep the differences in perspective. This is not an either/or situation. Why not include the best of both?*

53 *Preparation*
Curriculum for Team Leader Training

When a team leader faces a quality team for the first time, he or she had better be prepared to explain why the meeting was called, to involve everyone in decision-making, and to show the team how to get results. Those are the three basic components of a team leader training course: the mechanics of the company's quality process, how to run a meeting in a participative manner, and problem-solving techniques. Commercial packages are available and can be modified to reflect unique aspects of the company's quality process.

Every quality process has both philosophical and mechanical underpinnings, and a thorough knowledge of both is necessary. The foundation for the team leader training course should include material in the following areas: leadership (how the company encourages leadership at every level), customer focus (how to identify your customers), process improvement (how to focus on fixing processes, not people), and communications (how to convey the basics to your team), as well as how to use the support systems for the quality process (how to validate ideas, how to receive recognition, where to go for help). This last area is the one that will require the most customizing of an off-the-shelf training product.

Courses on participative team-leading often use a combination of lectures, group discussions, exercises, videotapes, and modeling to help attendees grasp the techniques. One of the most important—and most difficult—aspects to be taught is flexibility. For individuals whose experience in corporate meetings has been limited to one-way "information pushes" in which decisions were announced rather than discussed, this will represent a major change.

To run a meeting in a participative manner, encouraging everyone to contribute and take part, takes practice. The team leaders need to be made aware that not every one of their team members will be instantly comfortable as an active participant in discussions about how to do his or her job. Team members will buy in at different speeds, based on their own personalities, their degree of self-confidence with regard to their job knowledge and performance, and their past experience with various management fads.

Problem solving, the logical extension of a participative discussion, is also a blend of specific techniques and recognition of what the individuals involved in the conversation bring to the table. A knowledge of the wide variety of tools available coupled with an ability to be flexible will consistently yield the best results.

A too-common fault in some training courses is the insistence on a near-religious adherence to the specific steps of a complex problem-solving technique. It makes no sense to require that every single problem be analyzed using a "seven-step process" before a solution can be agreed upon. While it is obviously true that some problems do call for a multiple-step analysis with large amounts of data gathering and interim study prior to final resolution, it is equally obvious that other problems can be quickly cleaned up through what is essentially a one-step process: an agreement to "not do that anymore."

A refusal to acknowledge the difference in degree between various problems is tantamount to saying, "We do not want to work on any small problems." Few teams will be willing to tackle a problem where the solution process is more troublesome than just continuing to do "it" wrong.

Whether the organization builds its own team leader training course or begins with a commercial package, it is important that the course itself be the subject of continuous improvement. As team leaders change, there will be a need to re-offer the course, and the course that is taught to team leaders as year two of the company's quality process begins should not be the same course, with exactly the same materials, that was used to teach the first class of team leaders. The process will have evolved, the team leaders will have shared ideas on what worked particularly well (and what did not), and the incoming students will be more aware of what is at stake.

The need to update instruction dictates that the company "own" the course, even if that means buying local-use reproduction and amendment rights from the commercial source used as a starting point. Such an arrangement also makes it possible to make the particular mechanics of the company quality process (e.g., quality definitions, how to use the computer-based tracking program, the role of the "quality department," and the like) an integral part of the course.

Axiom #**53** *When evaluating training materials, ask yourself what you would want to know as a team leader. Then design your course accordingly.*

54 *Prototype*
A Quality School System

America as a whole can only achieve what its schools equip its citizens as individuals to achieve. And no one will deny that our schools are in trouble. When Motorola, winner of a 1988 Malcolm Baldrige National Quality Award, decides to locate a $600 million computer-chip operation in Japan because workers there have the necessary background in mathematics, the problem takes on a frightening immediacy.

For anyone tempted to despair, a look at the state of Kentucky is a powerful antidote. It has not as yet been called a "quality process," but what is happening in the Kentucky state school system bears a remarkable resemblance to a quality process in a service setting.

In common with many private sector quality efforts, the Kentucky school efforts were initiated in response to a crisis. In 1989, the Kentucky State Supreme Court declared that the way in which Kentucky funded its schools was unconstitutional because schools in poor neighborhoods were given significantly less money than those in wealthy districts. In a poor district, the spending per student was as low as $2238, while in the richer areas, it was as high as $5055.

Rather than construct some piecemeal approach that would get them through until the next crisis, the state leaders decided to seize the opportunity to make sweeping changes that would not only redress the spending differences but also fundamentally change the way the schools were run. The goal? Continuous improvement.

An article by Aaron Bernstein in *Business Week* magazine included this summary of the changes:[5]

KENTUCKY'S FORMULA FOR IMPROVED SCHOOLS

COUNCILS. Each school will be run by a council of three teachers, two parents, and the principal.

STANDARDS. By 1992, the state will define the key measures of student success, such as grades, attendance, and dropout rate.

RATING. In the 1994–5 school year, each school will be rated by its percentage increase of successful students vs. previous years.

REWARDS. After the ratings are completed, teachers in the most-improved schools will get bonuses of up to 15% a year.

SANCTIONS. Schools whose success rates fall by 5% or more will be taken over by the state. Its students can transfer if the decline continues.

The school councils can make decisions on curriculum, budgeting, staffing, and extracurricular activities. Each district has to have at least one school with a council by July 1, 1991; every school has to have a council by 1996.

Shirley Seever, the principal of an elementary school in rural Pendleton County, sounded like a business unit executive when she said, "We know more about what our kids need than people in Frankfort [the state capital]."

One of her teachers, Linda Thornton, picked up the theme when she said, "It puts an emphasis on the finished product, not on how many minutes a child spends in math class."

Some schools embraced the new opportunities for decision making quickly, according to Bernstein. He described how the Arlington Elementary School in Lexington reconfigured their student load to avoid having a mixed class of fourth- and fifth-graders. Because there were fewer fourth- and fifth-grade students than expected, one teacher had to transfer to another school, leaving two full fourth-grade classes, two full fifth-grade classes, and a mixed bag of fourth- and fifth-grade students.

Arlington's two special-education instructors "who teach mostly slow learners rather than severely disabled students" stepped into the breach:

> ... One special-ed teacher combined her seven students with a fourth-grade class. The other did the same with a fifth-grade one. This let Arlington avoid a split class. And with two teachers in the larger class, the student-teacher ratio in both grades is 23 instead of 28. The special-ed students haven't been hurt, since the school uses self-paced teaching methods, which let students work at their own speed. "We have the power now to change the things that stymie us from doing our jobs," says Tim Dedman, a fifth-grade teacher at Arlington.

Jim Parks of the State Education Department echoed the business-like vocabulary when he said, "We're equalizing their resources, setting performance goals for them and then getting out of their way. If they succeed, we reward them. If they fail, we sanction them. We have a lot of work to do to reach that point."

Axiom #54 *Business depends on education. America's business leaders, such as David Kearns, former CEO of Xerox and now Under Secretary of Education, and John Akers, CEO of IBM, have made education a priority. Both come from companies that have seen the positive impact of well-orchestrated quality processes.*

55 Provision
Quality à la Carte

*N*oel Cunningham and his wife Tammy own three restaurants in the Denver area: Strings, 240 Union Fish Market, and their newest venture, Ciao Baby.[6] Prior to opening Ciao Baby, Cunningham thought he would make some unusual provisions for the new venture. He was kind enough to talk about them and expand upon his philosophy of restaurant management in an interview:

Q. I understand Ciao Baby has only been open for four weeks. Could you describe the process of opening that restaurant?

A. First we hired the staff, then we held classes; but classroom training isn't the same as actually doing it. People kept asking me when I was going to open the restaurant; I kept telling them, "When it's ready." Once we got the building all ready, we had a bunch of "practice meals."

The first night, the kitchen crew and the front crew got to know each other, and the kitchen crew cooked just for them. The second night, we had 40 people come for dinner—employees of the other restaurants, good friends, folks like that. The third night, we had 70 people—loyal customers from the other two restaurants, folks like that; the fourth night, 120. All these meals were for free. The next day was Sunday and everyone had been under a lot of pressure so we took that day off. On Monday, we had another bunch in and had them fill out comment cards and pretend to pay so that we could get used to handling all those procedures.

Q. How long before you finally opened?

A. Not until we'd had seven nights of practice.

Q. Wasn't that expensive?

A. No. It was an investment. You only get one shot at getting things right; I wanted to make sure we got it right. During those practice dinners, I kept an eye on the kitchen, but I also tried to talk with every customer—to ask for their ideas and to ask them to please fill out their comment cards as honestly and completely as they could.

Q. What did you learn from those conversations and those comment cards?

A. Well, one thing we learned from the comment cards was that one guy didn't get his entree. And we put another printer in the kitchen, and we learned how to best set up a bus station, and we learned what they liked about our decor and our menu—hundreds of things. The nice part was that we learned all this and it wasn't at the customer's expense.

Q. What is your relationship with your suppliers? Are they a part of this?

A. My suppliers know that with me, it is quality first, service second, and price third. I talk with them a lot.

Q. Had you done this before—when you opened your other two restaurants, for instance?

A. No, I wasn't the majority owner back then. This is the first one that I've opened where Tammy and I were in control. We just think it is important to get things as right as possible before the cash registers are turned on.

Q. Do you mention "quality" in your ads?

A. We don't advertise. We would rather put the time and money into taking care of our customers. For instance, if we know that it is someone's birthday, we bring champagne and a cake to their table. Or, for one of our regular customers, every now and then we will have the waiter announce something like, "For every 3000 meals you purchase here, you get an evening for free—and this is your 3000th purchase here."

If someone brings a young child, we try to take the kid back to the kitchen about three-fourths of the way through the meal and have them scoop their own ice cream dessert. If it is their mother's birthday, then we'll have the kid help us decorate something for her—so the kid can take it back to the table. We accomplish a couple things. The kid was probably getting bored with eating by that time so the parents enjoy the break, plus the whole family can take pleasure in the specially decorated dessert.

Q. How big a staff do you have?

A. At Strings, about 70; at 240 Union, 55; and at Ciao Baby, 70. At staff meetings, I always remind them, I don't pay their paycheck, the customers do. They don't work for me, you see—we all work together. We have great team spirit.

Q. How do your employees get their ideas looked at?

A. We've got a very active suggestion program, plus I try to listen to them.

Q. For instance?

A. Last fall, the Broncos got off to a bad start so some DJ here in Denver climbed up on a billboard and vowed not to come down until they won a game. Well, they got off to a REALLY bad start and the poor guy was up there about six weeks. One Sunday, I was at Strings and a busboy who I knew was a big football fan came in and said, "Hey, that guy's going to finally get to come down—the Broncos are going to win!" "That's nice," I said. "We ought to have him here for his first meal," the kid said. "So, make it happen," I said. "What? How?" he said. "Heck, just call his radio station and invite him," I said.

Q. What happened?

A. The kid pulled it off! We had a party of 12 that night and we picked up the check. As it happened, the coach of the Broncos, Dan Reeves, was here and he sent over a bottle of champagne. It was a good time. Of course, the kid was a little worried at first when they told him that there would be 12 people coming, but I told him not to worry, that if you do things for the right reasons, everything will work out okay. As it turned out, the guy must have talked about us all the next morning on his radio show.

Q. Has your approach to opening Ciao Baby been a success? Was the money well spent?

A. When we had been open four weeks, we served over 400 people on a Saturday night. At Strings, it took us two years to get to that point. It wasn't expensive. It was one heckuva good investment.

A vendor/customer, Chuck DeLay of Rocky Mountain Hi (the company that supplies the T-shirts for all of Cunningham's restaurants) has this to say: "Noel is one of the best businessmen I know. He uses his customers to figure out how to attract more customers. And he certainly made my job easier. After dinner, I couldn't wait to design a new shirt. Of course, there was one small snag. I came up with six designs, and they all fit Ciao Baby so well that they had a tough time picking two. They asked me to keep the other four in reserve."

DeLay recognizes quality. Competing against approximately 1500 companies, Rocky Mountain Hi won the *Impressions Magazine* award for the best screen-printed T-shirt in 1990.

Axiom #**55** *Quality brings just deserts to all: customers, vendors, and providers.*

56 Recognition
Goldilocks and the Three Thank You's

Goldilocks was depressed. She felt guilty about having used the Three Bears' home for a rest and eating some of their food and taking a nap. Worse yet, she knew it was wrong to leave without saying "Thank you." Her mother had told her so.

She decided to square things by sending presents to each of the Three Bears—but what to get? All of them had contributed to her comfort (although she had liked the Baby Bear's contributions best), and she wanted to make sure that she gave each of the three something personal. She knew they deserved it. She also knew that she might want to sit in a rocker or take another nap someday. And she had really liked that third bowl of porridge.

What to give? For Poppa Bear, she settled on talking the local newspaper into printing a story about what a great bear he was. She figured that public recognition of his character and accomplishments would be just the thing.

On the same day that the story about Poppa Bear appeared in the paper, a package and an envelope arrived at the Bear residence, the former for Momma Bear and the latter for Little Baby Bear. Momma opened her package and found a lovely plaque with the engraved message "With thanks from Goldilocks to a GREAT BEAR—Momma Bear." Baby Bear opened his envelope and found a check for $25. Goldilocks had written "Thank you" in the lower left-hand corner of the check.

The Bears were not pleased. Poppa Bear was a very shy bear and was made uncomfortable by the newspaper story. Momma Bear already had all the plaques she needed. And Baby Bear knew that the check would be put in a bank somewhere for "his future." The dinner conversation was lively.

Poppa Bear said to Momma Bear, "You know, I'm sure that Goldilocks meant well, but I don't really like having my name splashed all over the paper. It would have been better if the whole family was featured. On the other hand, I could use a little money."

Momma Bear said, "I know what you mean. I know you don't really like that kind of publicity—even if you do deserve it—but I wouldn't have minded a story like that. It would have really felt good to see my name in print. I would have loved to have sent a copy to my mother."

Baby Bear, who had already turned his check over to his father, asked Momma Bear, "Can I have your plaque? Maybe we could have it changed to read 'Baby Bear.' "

They all agreed that it would have been very nice if Goldilocks had come to say thanks in person. Somehow, it seemed insincere for things to just show up out of the blue.

Goldilocks never was invited to the lovely little house in the forest. In fact, one day when she did venture into the woods to find the house, she found a sign on the door that read, "Goldilocks—Keep Out."

"Ingrates," she muttered, as she turned away. "I *said* 'thank you.' "

Axiom [#]**56** *Recognition is an integral part of quality. People hear "thank you" in different ways. What pleases the giver may not please the receiver, and the receiver's opinion is what counts. Solve the problem by saying thank you three or more ways to each person—and let the recipient respond to what tickles his or her fancy.*

57 *Reinforcement*

Getting Started
as a Team Leader

*D*ear Team Leader,

Congratulations! You've finished your Quality Team Leader training course. You've got your team. You've set a date for your first meeting. So now what?

Are you beginning to notice that there are a million other things to do besides this new "quality" thing? First, consider the time you are about to spend on the quality process as an investment. Like any other investment, it will hurt a bit up front, but the experience of hundreds of companies—and thousands upon thousands of people—is that the return is worth the effort.

The time you and your team put in now will be repaid manyfold in the coming months as you implement Quality Ideas to make your jobs better, both for your customers and for yourselves. Not only will you save time in the long run, but you will be able to clear up those hassles that currently make work an ordeal.

In preparing for your first meeting, you'll feel more confident if you spend some time with the Quality Idea Tracking Program to make sure that you have a working knowledge of its features. Another possibility is to do a little more reading on the topic. Honest, it is interesting—and there are lots of articles and books available.

For the first team meeting itself, there are several possible ways to get your team interested and involved: 1) describe the training you have received; 2) give the definitions of "Quality in Fact," "Quality in Perception," and "Customer," and invite discussion; 3) ask for help in listing all of the customers that you and your team members serve on a regular basis, and then, if it seems appropriate; 4) ask for a "brainstorm" list of possible areas to look at in the coming weeks and months (no solutions, just problems).

If you do make a list of customers, a way to proceed would be to ask the group, "Okay, which one do you want to start with? We'll get to all of these eventually, but where do you want to begin?"

Having decided on a customer (if you do decide on this approach), ask your team what they think are the customer's expectations—and if they differ in any way from the current specifications for your work. If possible, at a following meeting, invite several customers and ask them directly what their expectations are. Decide what to do about the gap between specifications and expectations. Sometimes the multistep problem-solving procedures that you have been taught will be appropriate. Other times the solution will be a matter of, "Well, why didn't you say so? We'll start doing that tomorrow." Rely on your good judgment.

If you are starting from a list of things to be improved, again emphasize that all of the items on the list will be considered in time. It is perfectly permissible to have more than one project going at one time. Try to identify everyone who is willing to take part in some improvement project.

It is probably a good idea to start with some relatively small ideas. Remember the advice given to an aspiring boxer on the key to a successful career: "Always pick somebody you can whip." Building some momentum will pay off down the line.

Initially, much of the team's enthusiasm and willingness to participate will depend on the attitude of the team leader. That, perhaps, is why you are called a "Team Leader" rather than a "team manager." This is an excellent opportunity to practice true leadership skills. Good luck . . . and have fun with it.

Axiom #57 *Formal team leader training is just the beginning. Team leaders deserve all the positive reinforcement they can get; after all, they are acquiring new skills for the company's benefit. On the practical side, such reinforcement can solidify lessons learned in the classroom.*

58 *Stability*

On the Vitality and Longevity of a Quality Process

*B*eware the quality consultant who cautions against expecting results early in a quality process. Beware the quality consultant who warns that results will slow as the process ages. Translated, what these phrases mean are, "Plan to pay me consultant fees for a long time," and "Don't blame me when your quality process peters out and dies."

Unfortunately, there are companies that turn these dire predictions into self-fulfilling prophecies before shrugging and looking for another HMI (Hot Management Idea). It does not have to be like that. A quality process can be amazingly stable. Carefully prepared and well initiated, a process can start quickly and with a bang; with ongoing support, it can make major contributions to a company's strength indefinitely.

Take the matter of preparation. It is not unusual for companies with successful quality processes to spend a year or more designing the process before its official launch. It takes time to investigate the alternatives, decide on options, train employees in techniques, make sure all employees receive orientation training, and set a structure (tracking program, recognition program, communications program, and so on) in place.

During that period, the company is already achieving results, although they remain essentially hidden. There are changes in corporate culture as the company struggles to accept new roles for managers and employees, new techniques, new goals. There is acknowledgement that quality is a journey, not a destination. This is reflected in a bit of semantics that all quality professionals tend to insist on: the difference between a program and a process.

A program, the wordsmiths say, is something that has a defined beginning and a defined ending point. It is something temporary by its very nature. A process is something that is ongoing, something that will be with the company until the walls come down. While there is a definite beginning, there is no ending. It is designed and intended to bring about permanent change and to be a continuing agent for change.

The importance of early intangible results of a quality process are rarely recognized except in retrospect. In the beginning, companies unfamiliar with a quality culture are more likely to be impressed with tangible results. They look for savings of time and money, volume of activity, increased sales, and a hundred other concrete measures as proof of the efficacy of quality. They are more likely to be impressed by the statistics at Paul Revere Insurance Group, Worcester, Massachusetts, where the first team logged on the tracking system 90 minutes after launch; where there were 120 to 140 implemented ideas per week for the first two years; where one idea alone saved $196,000; where one of the first Value Analysis workshops saved $618,700; where the company regained the number-one position in market share in their primary product after the first year.

None of these things could have happened without the subtle and sometimes not-so-subtle changes during the preparation phase. Companies that experience such early results from their quality processes earn them.

Sometimes the training phase itself identifies significant savings. Avatar International, a training company in Atlanta, Georgia, works on real-life situations rather than case studies and simulations in their training sessions. In its workshop with the 21 plant managers of Sewell Plastics Corp., headquartered in Atlanta, the participants had two boffo ideas. The first saved the company $518,000 in real dollars in the manufacture of their product; the second had potential savings of over $2 million in inventory-carrying costs.

Longevity of the quality process is another concern of many companies. Their experience with past programs leads them to believe that quality processes must have a limited natural life span. Part of that anxiety is allayed by adequate preparation. It also helps to realize that the quality process itself is subject to modification and revamping to keep it in touch with current realities. A continuous improvement process that did not itself continuously improve would be hypocritical.

Experience is the greatest reassurance. A quality process changes the way in which work gets accomplished. It sensitizes everyone to the possibilities for improvement and gives them the tools to achieve results. As long as the company maintains an environment in which a process can thrive, the possibilities are limitless.

One quality team leader was puzzled by a request to estimate when the team would run out of ideas: "Why should we run out? All we're doing is keeping up with, and trying to get a little bit ahead of, the world around us. So long as the company keeps getting new customers, and buying new equipment, and establishing new products and procedures, there's no way we can ever run out of ideas for improvement." The process at that company is eight years old.

Axiom #**58** *A process is quite different from a* program. *The first is designed to impact corporate culture—immediately and permanently. The second is an isolated event. Plan to be delighted with your* quality process *from the first—and to live with it happily ever after.*

59 Structure
A Blueprint for Matching Solutions to Problems

*O*rganizations of all types face three general categories of opportunities for improvement: continuous, periodic, and episodic. There can be (and is) overlap, but for purposes of discussion, continuous improvement deals with the question "Are we doing things right?"; periodic improvement evaluates "Are we doing the right things?"; and episodic improvement tries to define "Where did we go wrong—and what are we going to do about it?"

Employees at every level can address the question "Are we doing things right?" Continuous improvement requires a way for any employee to get a hearing for his or her ideas to improve quality—whether those ideas occur today or tomorrow or the day after tomorrow. This implies some formal structure both to capture ideas and to serve as the company's pledge to value employees' ideas whenever they occur.

Approaches to continuous improvement are varied and tend to reflect the amount of trust the top management of the organization is willing to extend to the people who work for them. The oldest and most common structure is the suggestion box. It is usually a passive system, calling for the lowest level of involvement on the part of the employee and leaving the concentration of power in the hands of management. With diligence and passion, even the hoary old suggestion box can be a treasury of ideas, but too often it is used merely as a gesture toward employee involvement.

Quality Circles were the initial attempt to bring the advantages inherent in teamwork to bear on problems inhibiting the quality of an organization. While a significant number of early successes were recorded, Quality Circles tended to have a disturbingly short half-life, usually caused in large part by the decision to involve only nonmanagement volunteers (in most cases about 10 percent of the workforce) and to retain all decision-making authority at the management level. Only the most enthusiastic took part—and even they tired after a while.

Quality Circles had another disadvantage. They were often constituted to address a single problem and disbanded when a solution was devised; continuous improvement virtually requires standing teams. The approach that is proving to have both impact and longevity is commonly called "Quality Teams." These teams, which can be either single-function or cross-functional, are found at all levels of an organization and are given carte blanche to exercise authority equal to their responsibility.

The most sophisticated model is self-managing work groups. In this case, the work group is given the responsibility and authority for determining everything from work schedules to hiring and firing. In return for that autonomy, they commit to achieving work goals agreed to with top management.

There is no one-size-fits-all quality process available. Nor is a company irrevocably committed to a particular system once they begin. For instance, a company could have begun in the mid-1980s with a Quality Circle program and moved on to the Quality Team approach.

Another opportunity to improve quality occurs at intervals. Periodic improvement arises on two occasions: when an organization is trying to decide whether the work processes currently in use are still viable (after a period of growth, for instance) and when a company is developing new products and services. Companies can anticipate dislocations associated with these events and prevent crisis situations. Meeting this challenge is also part of a well-designed quality effort.

For periodic opportunities, several methodologies exist. Two of the more common approaches—Value Analysis and Blueprinting—are discussed in the section *On Measurement*. What they have in common is that they are capable of either assessing the processes currently in place to see if they are still doing what they were intended to do (and whether or not a particular task is even needed anymore) or of creating new processes. Management is usually heavily involved in these efforts.

Despite everyone's best intentions, unforeseen problems do crop up. These episodes happen to an organization whether or not they have a quality effort under way, although the number of internal snafus will be smaller with a quality process, making the organization less vulnerable to problems in this category. The normal reaction to the emergence of an episodic "opportunity" is the formation of a team (or committee or task force) which is brought together for the sole purpose of resolving the situation. When a solution is put in place, the team disbands.

While a quality process does not prevent these episodes, it does contribute to their solution. In the context of a quality process, members of this one-time team bring to the table well-exercised skills in communications and problem solving; they are accustomed to sharing information and resources in an "everybody wins" atmosphere. When a quality process is in place, organizations are more alert to episodic events, and problems are solved more quickly and more permanently.

In every case, quality improvement depends on knowing what options are available and utilizing those that are appropriate. Quality by exhortation has a consistent track record: It does not work. There must be a specific structure to address problems. Precisely what structure is of less importance than that it be carried out in a constructive and consistent manner.

Companies that meet the full spectrum of quality challenges often refer to their efforts as Total Quality Management (TQM). Although the phrase Total Quality Management is somewhat inexact, everyone agrees that it includes having a coherent vision of the company and then using a variety of techniques—ranging from suggestion boxes to breakthrough thinking—to modify the company as it now stands and to envision the company of the future.

Axiom #**59** *The involvement and participation of every person on the payroll is necessary if a company is going to receive maximum benefit from a quality process. Exactly how that is achieved will vary, but in designing the company's quality process management must take into account all three types of quality opportunities: continuous, periodic, and episodic.*

60 *Synergy*
When the Whole Is Greater Than the Sum of Its Parts

When they lost to the Los Angeles Dodgers in the 1988 World Series, the Oakland Athletics repeatedly claimed that "the best team didn't win the World Series in '88." When they lost to the Cincinnati Reds in 1990, the Athletics broke out that same refrain. They were wrong both times.

If the Athletics were to change their assertion to "the best group of *individuals* didn't win the World Series in '88 or '90," few would offer an argument. In fact, following the 1990 Series (won in four straight games by Cincinnati), Reds player Todd Benzinger said, "The A's have the best talent in baseball, but we have the best team."

There is a penalty for acting as individuals in what is defined as a team sport. As Dave Stewart, Oakland's star pitcher, said after the 1990 World Series, "Winning feels better than most people think, and losing feels worse."

What the Dodgers and Reds each achieved by acting as a team could not have been predicted by the individual performances of the teams' players. They "played above their heads"; they also won.

So it is in business.

It is quite possible that if, for instance, individuals on the General Motors payroll were matched, one-to-one, against the individuals on the Toyota payroll, that GM would do very well in the comparisons. Education, years of experience, proven (off the job) creativity, and desire to be a functioning part of a winning organization ... American employees and managers stack up favorably against any other national group.

Yet Toyota models consistently occupy the top slots in quality assessments while GM was reduced to bragging publicly that Buick was Number 5 in 1990. In large part, this is the same thing that happened to Oakland in 1988 and 1990—inspired teams beat collections of individuals.

This is not to say that all you need is a strong feeling of teamwork and success will be assured. There are conditions under which sheer talent will win out. Consider the Boston Red Sox in their bid for the World Series in 1990. Against their league rivals the Toronto Bluejays, the Boston Red Sox were the inferiors, taken on a position-by-position basis. By being a team, however, and filling in each other's weakness, they defeated the Bluejays to earn a shot at the Athletics. Then they ran into a stone wall. The Athletics were able to defeat the Red Sox even without being a cohesive team. Sometimes the sum of individual strengths is overwhelming. Teamwork maximizes potential, but the potential must be there.

Axiom #**60** *The best combination is talent and teamwork. As a duo, its synergy is hard to beat—as GM will attest. After a sustained effort to build a culture of teamwork and customer awareness—and thanks to the investments and long-term commitment of top management—GM's Cadillac Division won the Malcolm Baldrige National Quality Award in 1990.*

61 Teamwork

The Ultimate Question for Quality: What Can We Do Together?

*J*eff Pym observed the quality process at his company, Paul Revere of Canada, and concluded that a quality process grows through three stages:

> What can you do for me?
> What can I do for me?
> What can I do for you?

He is not alone in his observation. Many companies have watched as employees—including management—initially look at a quality process as a way to make suggestions on how *other* employees can improve *their* performance. It takes awhile for a basic truth to set in: Quality is about what *I* can do to improve *my* performance.

In this second phase, employees often use the petty irritations of their work as a source of ideas on how to improve quality. What is inconvenient for me? What do I think is a waste of time? Success in handling these situations engenders confidence and can be translated into a more sophisticated appreciation of how customers are impacted by corporate processes and policies. The stage is set for the "What can I do for you?" phase of a quality process.

Joe McConville, Director of Quality at Paul Revere Insurance Group, Worcester, Massachusetts, in the fourth year of their Quality Has Value process, added a corollary to Pym's Phases:

> What can we do together?

This corollary was based on the discovery that over 90 percent of the ideas that teams were working on that year had a goal based on customer communications. Over 50 percent of the ideas had a training goal, either for team members to upgrade their own skills or for the team to aid their customers—often other teams—in acquiring new skills through informal corporate training. The following three pages are excerpts from a flyer put out by the PROFits Quality Team offering their expertise to train other teams.

FLASH:

Q PARTNERS SOUGHT

Love Connection, Move Over: PROFits Quality Partners Available

The PROFits Quality Team today announced that it is implementing a new Partnership Program as part of its Quality efforts for 1989. The program, designed to pair PROFits consultants with interested Quality Teams throughout the company, will take effect in January of 1989 at the start of the new Quality year.

The PROFits are a Quality team made up of members from the Information Center, IS Planning, and IS Research. The theory behind the new Partnership Program is that team members can bring some specific skills — like expertise in a particular software package, systems and data analysis, writing and training skills, for example — to a team that might have Quality projects in mind that would benefit from those skills. In return, the partner team will help the PROFits analyst to learn more about the various business areas of the company, so that they're better able to meet end-user computing needs in the future.

Program Guidelines Outlined

While PROFits team members will be full participating members of the Quality teams they're partnered with, the PROFits will remain a team itself. They'll be measured by the success of their partner teams — so if you don't look good, they don't look good.

There will be a few ground rules that PROFits team members and their partner teams will be asked to follow. For example, while a PROFits analyst may be a whiz with PROFS and document formats, his or her job will be to consult with a team in that area — not develop actual products for them.

Following Pages:

Personals
Advice
Classified

Dear Santa,

I have been good all year. I have accomplished all my Quality team goals and have gone GOLD each quarter. I learned the Interactive Chart Utility to help my friends prepare displays for the Qualifest. I studied SAS and Dynaplan so I could answer questions at the HELP Desk. I worked hard to use DCF to make my documents easier to read. I hope that you agree that I deserve to be rewarded for my good behavior. Please bring me a Quality team that I can be on in 1989. I promise to be even better next year. Love, "Virginia"; Route 178-00, Ad #6.

Results-oriented IC analyst seeking new and different challenges. Negative, stubborn, inflexible, and demanding, but I'm worth the effort. I'll call your problems the way I see them, and I'll also deliver solutions that make sense. Write 178-00, Ad #13.

Desperately Seeking Gold!

Gold Miner seeks team with untapped resources (ideas for applications). I'll find the mother lode with my prospecting skills (years of IC systems analysis skill) and I'll mine it with my tools (SAS, Dynaplan, Chart Utility ...). Stake your claim by responding to the "Old Prospector" 178-00, Ad #1 — you won't get the shaft.

DI Quality Teams Take Note

Are you and your teammates unfulfilled ... information wise?

Have your experiences left you wanting ... for better DI reports?

Perhaps an experienced performer can help! An understanding of available DI data and access to tools might be just what you need. Maybe you're doing things the hard way. Let's talk. If you're interested, write 178-00, Ad #7.

IC Systems Analyst seeks the partnership of an enthusiastic Quality Team, possible relationship. Interested in all areas of the company. I have a good sense of humor, like sports, and enjoy a challenge. If you're honest and looking for some expertise in PROFS, DCF, etc., let's be friends. I'll answer all replies, but you have to answer this ad first. Write — Route 178-00, Ad #4.

Analyst seeks opportunity to reexamine workflow. I need to learn what your department does, and who knows, maybe I can ID some opportunities. Especially interested in Group but Individual is interesting too. Other interests include training, snakes, graphics and gardening. Let's take a chance on each other and see what happens from there. Respond Route 178-00, Ad #11.

Systems Analyst, 26 but looks 36, seeks Quality team for creative partnership. Into graphics, technical and promotional writing, and long walks through Filene's. If you're interested in some discreet consultations in slidemaking computer graphics, desktop publishing or any other presentation technologies, I'm interested in a trade: training in those areas for lessons from experienced Paul Revere marketeers. Respond in confidence to Route 178-00, Ad #3. No freaks.

22 Days 'til Quality '89.
Get your consultant now.

NEW YEAR'S SPECIAL

PROFS

Four Exciting Classes!
January 20, 23, 24, & 26th

*Call X5218 for Class Times
and Location.*

Advice
Gabriella van User

Yo Gabby:

My password has expired again, and I don't know how much more I can take. What should I do? Signed,
End of My Rope

Dear Rope:

You need help in this difficult time. Call extension 5218. Please, let me know what happens. I care.

Yo Gabby:

I hope you'll print just one more letter about an awful problem. No matter what font I use, every time I try to print my document I get the message "Text Exceeds Right Page Boundary". What should I do? Signed,
DCF Dreader

Dear Dreader:

You need help. I urge you to call the Help Desk at extension 5218. And please, let me know what happens. I care.

*Excerpts from a newsletter
PROFits Quality Team
Paul Revere Insurance Group
December 1988*

Axiom *#***61** *Never underestimate the power of teamwork to improve quality. It can also be fun.*

62 Vocabulary
A Short Dictionary
of Quality Terms

*E*very vocation or specialty has its own vocabulary, its own particular way of using even ordinary words. The same is true with quality. When McCormack and Dodge, a mainframe software and software services company in Natick, Massachusetts, launched its Quality Without Limits process, its director published a dictionary of terms that reflected M&D's approach: 100 percent employee participation on Quality Teams supplemented by additional management participation in Value Analysis workshops. Slightly modified, the dictionary appears below. It can be used by any organization beginning a similar quality process:

Customer. Anyone to whom you (personally, your department, or the company) provide service, product, or information. For many, their primary customer(s) will be other employees.

Incentives. Not a part of the quality process. There is no attempt to "buy" anyone's participation; the employees of a company are worth far more than could be afforded. There will be a sincere effort at saying "thank you" for participation in the process.

Kaizen. A Japanese word meaning the philosophy of continuous improvement. Also, the title of a very good book by Masaaki Imai.

Quality. The result of the combination of two interlaced concepts: Quality in Fact and Quality in Perception. Also, it is the competitive edge that will help to insure that a company not only survives but succeeds.

Quality Idea. Any idea, large or small, considered by a Quality Team working to improve whatever it is that the team is responsible for accomplishing. Implementation of an idea does not mean that there was necessarily anything wrong before; it is possible to go from good to better—or even from better to best.

Quality Idea Analyst. The "mechanics" of the quality process; always available to talk with any Quality Team Leader. Primary function is to certify Quality Ideas and insure that all Quality Teams receive deserved recognition/gratitude. If not able to immediately answer a question or provide requested help, an analyst will be able to find it and provide it in a very short time.

Quality Idea Tracking Program. A software program that makes it easy for Quality Teams to keep a log of their progress and for the Quality Idea Analysts to track completion of ideas. Once an idea is noted as implemented on the QITP, the team leader will be contacted by a Quality Idea Analyst—so that the idea can be certified.

Quality in Fact. Meeting specifications as they are understood; achieved when a person does his or her job as he or she believes it should be done.

Quality in Perception. Achieved when someone else believes that what is being offered will meet their expectations, that it will do or be what they want. The key to quality is to insure that specifications meet the expectations of the customer. If they do not, the gap must first be recognized and explained, and then worked on, either by changing the specifications or educating the expectations.

Quality Team. A group of 6 to 12 employees—normally people who work together on a day-to-day basis—who meet regularly to discuss methods to improve the quality of whatever it is that they do. Their efforts are made possible by the granting of authority commensurate with responsibility. As the months go by, many of these teams will become cross-functional as groups of employees invite other employees who are their customers to join their team.

Quality Team Leader. The leader of a group of employees attempting to improve the quality of whatever it is that they do; the Quality Team Leader is trained in the quality process and in how to conduct a meeting in a participative, problem-solving manner. (For many, the second part of the training will be as much a refresher as it is new material.) Quality Team Leaders will be the primary activists in the effort to put the company on the road to a philosophy of continuous improvement.

Recognition/Gratitude/Celebration. An indispensable piece of the quality process. Efforts to say "thank you" to every deserving Quality Team will be frequent and varied.

Task Force. A group of employees that may be cross-functional and/or cross-level, depending upon the problem that serves as a catalyst for their formation. This temporary team will normally disband once a solution is agreed to and implementation assured.

Value Analysis. A program that is an integral portion of the quality process. Working with a trained facilitator, a department will take an in-depth look at their functions and processes. Recommendations that result from a Value Analysis Workshop will be the sole property of the workshop participants, not the workshop facilitator.

Why. The quality process is being launched because the president and the top management team sincerely believe that quality will give the company a competitive edge in future years and that the employees of this company are talented adult business people who want the company to succeed and who are capable of establishing an atmosphere of continuous improvement.

Axiom #**62** *Whatever approach a company chooses for a quality process, a common vocabulary will be necessary to communicate goals and methods effectively.*

Part Three
On Measurement

63 Absolutes
Management Philosophers Speak

When you can measure what you are speaking about, and express it in numbers, you know something about it; but when you cannot measure it, when you cannot express it in numbers, your knowledge is of a meager and unsatisfactory kind: it may be the beginning of knowledge, but you have scarcely, in your thoughts, advanced to the stage of *science*.
　　　　—*William Thomson, Lord Kelvin*
　　　Popular Lectures & Addresses [1891–1894]

If you don't know where you are going, you might end up someplace else.　　　　　—*Lawrence Peter [Yogi] Berra*

Axiom #**63** *One of the absolutes of quality is that you can't manage what you can't measure. Measurement tells you where you are and where you are going.*

64 Accessibility
A Paperboy Named Pareto and How He Developed His Analysis

*Y*oung Pareto, the neighborhood paperboy, noticed that every so often his bundle of papers was delivered "late." Since he arrived at the dark, cold corner each morning at precisely the same time, not having the papers there when he arrived was most unpleasant and inconvenient.

He decided to keep track of actual delivery time for a few weeks. Since he didn't care how early the papers came as long as they were waiting for him, he marked all such occasions as simply "OK" on his score sheet. When he was there before the papers were, however, he recorded the exact time that they were finally dropped at his freezing feet.

He soon confirmed what he suspected: The papers were rarely late by more than 5 minutes on Monday through Friday and always 30 to 40 minutes late on Saturdays. So far as the variation of up to 5 minutes on Monday through Friday, Pareto decided that it was likely that such variables as traffic and weather were at play. The one late weekday delivery outside the 5-minute variance had been explained by a late-breaking news story the night before that had justified "holding the presses."

He thought it was interesting that the ratio of on-time papers to late papers was 5 to 1, or roughly 80 percent to 20 percent. (He didn't deliver the Sunday paper; another kid had been doing that route for years.)

A phone call to the newspaper office downtown revealed that there was a different driver on Saturdays. The Saturday driver left the central office at the same time as the Monday through Friday driver—the dispatcher made sure of that—but he had a slightly different route.

The budding statistician decided that he had two choices, either sleep an extra 30 minutes each Saturday morning or ask the Saturday driver to make a change in the route and get to his corner earlier. The deciding factor: whether or not his customers cared. As far as Pareto was concerned, the extra sleep was an attractive option.

While making his collections that week, Pareto asked his customers if receiving their paper 30 minutes later on Saturday mornings presented a problem. The customers were unanimous in agreeing that it did not.

Pareto benefited from his analysis. He got a little more sleep on the weekends from then on, and he even noticed that his weekly tips were a bit bigger. Customers were delighted to have a paperboy who asked them when they wanted their paper delivered. It had never happened before.

Axiom #**64** *Pareto Analysis (also called the 80-20 Rule) is a popular and useful measurement tool for identifying and prioritizing problems. This technique is readily accessible: Pareto Analysis need not be mysterious.*

65 *Alert*

Tripwire Measurement: An Early Warning System

*F*rom the first time that humans suspected that trouble might sneak up on them, tripwires have been used. They have a very specific, but limited, purpose. A tripwire tells you that there is trouble nearby and tells you approximately where to look.

In the case of a troop of Scouts expecting a raid by a neighboring group during a Jamboree, a literal tripwire may be strung across a likely path and attached either to a noisemaker or to someone's toe. In a coal mine, a canary is a tripwire measurement for poisonous gases. If the canary dies, miners know there is a problem. For most parents, a child's temperature serves as a tripwire measurement. If the child's temperature is normal, all is assumed to be well, barring other overwhelming evidence. If there is a fever, on the other hand, the alarm is sounded. Little specific information is gleaned—only that something needs attention.

More complex tripwires also find their way into everyday usage. A new tripwire is currently being put in place for use by parents of college-age offspring. As soon as the last legal battle is fought, colleges will be required to publish both their graduation rates and their on-campus crime rates. Neither will tell a parent or a prospective student specifically what to do, but both will indicate what further information might be worth seeking out.

It is hoped that business tripwires are at least as sophisticated as the graduation and crime statistics in their make-up, but the result of all tripwires is the same: a not-particularly-precise alert. A tripwire is a relatively low-cost diagnostic tool that signals an organization that a problem exists without immediately solving anything. With the airlines, the on-time and baggage-lost statistics released monthly serve as tripwires. The fact that an airline's on-time rate dips from one month to the next doesn't really tell management anything about what solutions might be appropriate. It does, however, tell them that there is a problem, and it tells them in which direction they should focus their efforts.

A well-designed set of tripwires makes it possible to apply constrained resources where most needed. No organization can monitor all contingencies all the time. The expenditure of resources would bring the company to its knees in short order.

Encamped armies often set tripwires at various distances from the heart of the camp. The devices don't stop the invaders, but they do give the defenders advance notice of an intruder's arrival. The farther away the impending trouble can be identified, the more time the leadership has to decide what to do about it and the better chance they have of committing exactly the right resources to "solve the problem." Such an economical employment of people and material allows them to have something left to face the next crisis.

The same is true in business. The more sensitive the tripwires, the farther out they are, the more precise the company can be in deploying its resources to prevent severe problems and the more capable it will be of handling more than one problem at a time. Rather than measuring every possible step of every possible process, a series of tripwires helps to define when more elegant (or complicated) Statistical Process Control options—or simply more attention by people capable of solving the problem—need to be activated.

Tripwire measurement is a defense against surprises. Unfortunately, as with all forms of measurement, it is only as good as the people operating the system. No measurement is a sure protection against bad decisions. It's a good bet that the defenders of Troy had tripwires in place—and dismantled them in order to pull that big, lovely wooden horse inside the gates.

Axiom #**65** *A few well-chosen measures can alert a company to a problem that requires attention.*

66 Awareness
Find the Wheel Before It Squeaks

*J*ust as virtually all machines seem to work better if they are taken apart and greased every so often, so too with the relationship between suppliers and customers. The best "lubricant" for both noisy and silent wheels is customer service and follow-up. All too often, though, only the squeaky wheel gets the grease. The result can be an untimely breakdown.

In the late 1970s, the Tennant Company, headquartered in Minneapolis, Minnesota, was doing well. The maker of floor-finishing equipment was a leader in its industry, and no wheels were squeaking.

Then their new Japanese customers began complaining. The Japanese claimed that Tennant machines leaked. The Tennant management couldn't understand it. They'd made and sold a lot of machines in the United States over the years, and nobody had ever voiced that complaint before.

Their interest in pursuing the Japanese complaints was heightened in 1979 when Toyota announced that it was considering entering the floor-finishing equipment market. As Roger Hale, president of Tennant, has since said, "If you want a wake-up call, just have Toyota announce it is coming into your niche."

Something needed to be done about the problem in Japan. To try to get a better handle on what might be happening, the Tennant management decided to check with their American customers who had been silent on the subject—their quiet wheels. To their surprise—and shock—they found out that the machines purchased by their American customers also leaked but, "We just wipe it up."

For whatever reason, American consumers—both at the corporate and personal level—tend not to complain until the situation is serious. Rather, they suffer along until a more attractive alternative presents itself, and then they move—permanently—to a new source for the service or product in question.

When the people of Tennant first began the discussion in their plant in Minneapolis as to what to do about the problem (a "leak" was defined as "one drop of oil falling from a hydraulic joint during one hour of machine operation at normal operating temperature and pressure"), one engineer recommended putting a large drip pan under each machine. That helped to convince the company leadership that changes in thinking as well as changes in operation were needed.

A quality process was initiated, training began, and measurements were taken to determine a baseline from which to begin. On average, Tennant found it could expect one leak for every 75 joints assembled. Since the typical machine had 150 joints, they were averaging 2 leaky joints per machine. While most of these were caught before the machine left the company floor, even those that were found required rework, a cost in both materials and time.

Data were collected and used to guide improvement efforts, resulting in steady progress. This was reflected in the year-by-year statistics of leaky joints during the first 10 years of the Tennant quality process:

1979—one leak per   75 joints
1980—one leak per 100 joints
1981—one leak per 216 joints
1982—one leak per 509 joints
1983—one leak per 611 joints
1984—one leak per 619 joints
1985—one leak per 1286 joints
1986—one leak per 2800 joints
1987—one leak per 3233 joints
1988—one leak per 4804 joints

In August 1985, Tennant began surveying all their customers, asking if they had had any difficulties with their machines. There were no leaks reported from the field during 1985 and 1986. Toyota did not enter the field, and Tennant's sales and market share have grown steadily.

Axiom *#**66*** *Had it not been for the squeaky wheels in Japan, Tennant may not have been made aware of their eroding popularity in their biggest market until their customers began walking away. The opinion of customers must be aggressively sought out—even in the absence of complaints.*

67 Benchmarks

Mirror, Mirror, on the Wall . . . Who's the Fairest in My Market Sector?

*O*nce upon a time, benchmarking was easy. One of the first recorded cases, albeit rudimentary, involved a stepmother and queen who periodically asked her magic mirror, "Mirror, mirror, on the wall, who's the fairest of them all?"

By frequently checking herself against the competition in the only category to which she gave value, she was able to reassure herself as to her Number 1 position for a number of years. In retrospect, she should probably have gone into the matter in more depth. She might have asked her mirror probing questions, such as, "Who is Number 2, how quickly is she gaining, and what can I do about it?"

Had the evil stepmother's methods been more sophisticated, perhaps she could have avoided going the poisoned apple route (clearly a desperate move) to regain her position as the unquestioned fairest in the land. As it was, her response to bad news didn't do her reputation as a wife and parent a bit of good.

But, if not the apple, what other options did she have? For one, had the queen asked more detailed questions to find out exactly what the competition had going for it, she could have elicited specifics on her own perceived and real strengths and weaknesses. If she were unable to hold off the competition, she might have used the mirror to carve out a particular niche ("Who's the fairest in my age group?") or to check out new markets ("Who's the fairest in each of the neighboring kingdoms? How do they compare to me?").

The queen should be given some credit for not looking around for a new mirror, one that would give her the answer she wanted to hear. To do so would have freed her from the need to do anything at all in response to her rival's growing reputation. Of course, it would also have assured that she didn't get the bad news about being Number 2 until she was, let's say, Number 15 and the situation was even more unpleasant.

The thoughtful use of benchmarking, the use of all kinds of questions and the resultant information, has grown into a valuable and increasingly popular tool to gauge and improve quality. Traditional measurement of market share is suggestive of "who's the fairest of them all" and is only a very basic type of benchmarking. More sophisticated methods yield better results.

After deciding on a major quality effort—one that led to a Malcolm Baldrige National Quality Award in 1989—the Xerox

Corporation made benchmarking an important part of its activities. It looked at its own industry and, where necessary because of the lack of competition or because they were already Number 1 in a particular category, went outside its confines to find standards to shoot for.

In the area of handling telephone calls and responding to customer requests, for instance, they chose mail-order retailer L.L. Bean as their competitor/teacher. Even though Xerox will never compete directly against L.L. Bean, they honed that particular component of their overall procedures to meet the perceived "best in class." Their reasoning was that if they could match L.L. Bean, then they would obviously be the best in their own industry.

Benchmarking involves establishing goals based on real experience—yours or someone else's—and then striving to reach, and surpass, those marks . . . even if the only person or organization left to beat is yourself.

Axiom [#] **67** *Benchmarking—the process of measuring an organization's or an individual's current status and comparing it either to past performance or to the accomplishments of others— is a good common-sense first step to improving quality.*

68 *Catalysts*
Surveys? What Do You Think?

*I*n the context of improving quality, there are three primary types of surveys:

- Surveys of external customers designed to learn what they think about a particular service or product
- Surveys of employees in their roles as internal customers designed to learn what they think about the service or

product that they receive from other units within the organization

- Surveys of employees' attitudes designed to learn what they think about the organization itself

With all three types of surveys, certain rules are applicable if maximum advantage is to be realized:

- Surveys must be repeated on a regular basis. The reason for the survey is the same as for any other form of measurement—to serve as a source of ideas for future action and to track progress. Without a regular schedule of surveys, these two basic benefits are minimized.
- Results of the survey must be communicated to the appropriate people. These "appropriate people" are the folks who completed the survey and the folks who can do something about the answers. In the case of surveys of internal customers, common sense should dictate the sharing of results. No one but the members of the department that is rated lowest need know that their department has the most work to do. On the other hand, the departments that score highest deserve public recognition. In the case of the attitude surveys, the employees deserve to know the results— so that individuals can find out if their opinion is in the majority or not.
- There needs to be a plan for reacting to the surveys. It is useless to ask questions in hopes that you'll get the "right" answer; there must be an intent to react if the "wrong" (or unexpected) answer pops up. With internal customer surveys, the top management plan need be nothing more than "to give the results to the department heads and tell them when the next survey will be conducted." For the attitude surveys, one approach is to set a threshold and determine to address any question the answer to which falls beneath that threshold. For instance, "If less than 70 percent of the organization believes that a particular policy is equitable, a cross-functional and cross-level task force

will be initiated to address the issue and make recommendations to the executive council."

Surveying need not be complex. Informal surveying occurs within an organization every time any employee asks another, "Do you use this service or product? How could it be made more useful for you?" as part of routine conversation. While the habit of talking to each other works, it has shortcomings when attempting to document progress.

A simple, formal survey can be very effective. One approach to surveying internal customers is a survey devoting one page to each department bearing a standard set of questions common to every department (e.g., how accurate are they? how timely are they?) plus a few additional questions peculiar to each department (as defined by the department management). Employees can then answer questions only for departments with which they deal personally. When administered periodically, such a survey focuses employee efforts and makes it possible to chart progress.

Surveys can be as short as one question. A manager who is looking for ideas on what next to improve need only give all those who work for him or her this one-question survey: "The things that prevent me from doing my job right the first time are: . . ." The employees should be given a couple of days to return the survey.

The same rules apply to a one-question survey. That is, the question should be asked on a regular basis, the answers should be shared with the appropriate people, and there needs to be a plan devised for dealing with the results. As with larger, more formal surveys, don't ask the question if you are not prepared to respond to the "wrong" answer.

The wording of surveys can itself be a powerful message. At the Paul Revere Insurance Group, for instance, all sales offices are required to fill out and submit on a monthly basis a survey concerning the performance of the home office during the preceding month. The objective is to find out how well the people in the home office are serving one of their most important customers.

The heart of the survey consists of two questions: "What went wrong during the past month?" and "Who did something particularly well for you in the past month?" The answers allow the home office management to focus corrective efforts on processes, while at the same time identifying the specific individuals deserving of gratitude for their actions in support of their customers and the company.

Surveying must be aggressive. Much more is learned from seeking out respondents and asking them specific questions (in addition to allowing open-ended responses) than from "Please fill this in and mail it if you're really mad" cards. The latter helps to identify the squeaky wheels; the former goes after the far more numerous quiet wheels.

Aggressive surveying can also save money while raising quality. One service organization initiated a program of having its employees call their sales offices on a regular basis just to see if there was anything that needed attention. It was anticipated that the program would significantly increase the department's phone bill, but the consensus was that the money spent would be recouped in intangible ways, such as a better relationship between the field and the headquarters.

In fact, the program not only improved the relationship but also reduced the phone bill. A single phone call that uncovered and headed off a problem proved to be cheaper than several tense phone calls once the problem had erupted.

All surveying has economic implications. Surveys of external customers can take several forms from focus groups to written questionnaires, but the aim is always the same: to understand the expectations of the people who are most likely to buy the company's service or product. The objective of a particular survey may be to assess a current service or product, to compare it to that of a competitor, or to test the potential of a service or product still in the conceptual stage. Whatever the stated objective, the underlying question is "How likely are you to give us some (more) money in the near future?"

Surveys of internal customers are not as clearly related to the bottom line, although there is a kind of currency—good will. The underlying question here is "How likely is the next transaction between employees within a company to go quickly and smoothly?" The answer to that question has a dollar value.

Surveys designed to measure the attitude of the employees toward the organization yield information that can help solve stubborn problems such as absenteeism and turnover, both of which have economic impact.

Axiom #**68** *Measurements are taken as a catalyst for change. Not all measurements, however, are taken with a set of calipers. Surveys are also a valid, and valuable, means of measurement.*

69 Cooperation
A Fairy Tale of Faulty Interaction

*O*nce upon a time, a young woman was hired for a new job because the king had heard her father declare that she was the best spinner in the kingdom. She was nervous and excited. She knew that she was pretty good—but the best? Time would tell.

Her first interview with the king had gone fairly well. He had explained that the cloth from their kingdom was selling so well that "it might as well be made of gold," and he welcomed her by personally showing her a brand new spinning wheel. It seemed like an excellent start, and she eagerly began to spin.

Her optimism was somewhat blighted by the unfamiliarity of the wheel and the appearance of a strange little man with a caliper in his pocket and a manual under his arm who introduced himself as Rumpelstiltskin. She didn't understand his exact position in the kingdom, but he told her that it was because of him the cloth from their kingdom had such a good reputation. He told her how much thread to make and promised to return the next evening to inspect her work.

Her second interview with Rumpelstiltskin was anything but pleasant. She had struggled to produce the amount of thread required and thought the outcome was rather good. Rumpelstiltskin was not impressed. He looked at her work with disdain and querulously demanded, "You call this good work? This may be all right where you come from, but it is far below our standards."

"Is it?" she timidly replied. "I can't see what's wrong with it."

"We can't use it," sniffed Rumpelstiltskin.

"Maybe if you could explain exactly what is wrong, I could fix it," the puzzled young lady repeated quietly. "I really would like to try," she apologized.

Rumpelstiltskin handed her a couple of samples and a manual. "Your answer is in here," he intoned and promised to visit her the following evening.

The young woman found that after she read the manual she could spin thread that looked exactly like the sample. True, there were times when she had to stop and wait for Rumpelstiltskin to appear because no matter what she tried, her spinning wheel refused to cooperate. He grudgingly agreed that it was better to wait until adjustments could be made to her wheel than to continue to produce thread that could not be used. Overall, things looked bright.

The next crisis came unexpectedly. The king came in very excited. "You, my dear," he enthused, "are a miracle worker. Orders for the cloth made from your thread are pouring in. You must increase your output immediately!" He left skipping down the hall. It sounded like good news, but the young woman could see several problems.

That evening when Rumpelstiltskin appeared, the young lady relayed the conversation with the king. She knew that she couldn't always afford to sit and wait for Rumpelstiltskin to appear and solve her problems. She wanted him to show her how to fix her wheel. She also had a few ideas for increasing the amount of thread but knew it would take cooperation from the dyers and weavers.

Rumpelstiltskin didn't even listen to her. Although he and the young woman were by now on very good terms (after all, had not the king complimented him on how well his protégée was doing?), he appeared affronted. "Don't you worry your pretty little head about this," he cut her off. "This is my job."

"But I'm the one who's going to get blamed if the order isn't filled," she started to protest. "Couldn't we work together on this?"

"This is a very complex problem," he interrupted tersely. "You do very well at the wheel, but you haven't been trained to deal with this." When she didn't look convinced, he became incensed. "Look, it isn't as if I'm asking for your first-born child," he shouted. "I just want you to remember your job is your job, and my job is mine."

That evening the young woman explained her dilemma to her father. "I feel as if I'm stuck in the middle," she sighed. "The king keeps dreaming about the gold he could get from increased sales and can't seem to understand that it is going to be very difficult to spin more thread unless we make major changes. Rumpelstiltskin acts as if he's the only one who could possibly understand the problem, let alone solve it, and he resents any suggestions. What am I going to do?"

As it turned out, she had no opportunity to do anything. Rumpelstiltskin tried desperately to redirect everyone's efforts, but since he wouldn't share any real information, the workers throughout the kingdom became confused. Production fell. Orders were lost. One day, after a particularly acrimonious conversation with the young woman, Rumpelstiltskin slammed out of the castle and was never seen again.

Axiom #**69** *Quality and cooperation are inseparable in measurement, just as they are in leadership and participation. Beware the "Rumpelstiltskin Complex": quality control specialists who act as if their discipline is too arcane and complex for mere mortals. Quality control is most effective when it is designed into production processes for the use of employees at every level. Everyone can help with both the design and the implementation of quality control.*

70 Customer Focus
What Did You Expect?

It looks like we are meeting our new specifications.
—Krocodil, *USSR*

Axiom #**70** *Here is a case in clear violation of Dr. Joseph Juran's definition of quality, "Fitness for use." As an alternative, satisfying this three-part definition of quality would have prevented the problem:*

- *Quality in Fact—Meeting your own specifications.*
- *Quality in Perception—Meeting your customers' expectations.*
- *Customer—Anyone to whom you provide product, service, or information.*

71 Design

Cafeteria Customer Service: Put Your Money Where Their Mouth Is

An article tucked into the back page of the *Worcester Telegram and Gazette* told the story of an unusual customer service guarantee:[1]

> If the food on campus is hard to swallow, the price won't be.
>
> That's a promise from Clark University [Worcester, Massachusetts], where a money-back guarantee will be added to the dining-hall menu Monday when students return from semester break.
>
> Clark and its food-service contractor, Daka Inc., will refund a student the price of a meal if the diner's tastes cannot be satisfied. The student's account would be credited $1.66 for breakfast, $3.32 for lunch or brunch, or $4.99 for dinner.
>
> College food gets a bad rap, said Clark business manager Jack Foley. Students everywhere "write home about the quality of the food. But what students really want is value for their dollar," he said.
>
> Daka sees the guarantee as a way to elicit specific criticisms rather than general whining, said vice president Ron Cohen. "Some-

times our biggest problem is customers don't come up and tell us what's bothering them." Then kitchen managers are left to guess where improvements are needed, he said.

At Clark, the money-back offer coincides with the opening of a new, 400-seat dining hall and expanded meal hours. Daka served a free lunch yesterday to the faculty and staff to celebrate. "It was really good food," said Clark spokeswoman Kate Chesley, who had a cheeseburger, french fries, salad, and chocolate milk. She said the new hall is set up to offer more choices, so Clark and Daka are confident enough to bank on pleasing palates. The school and the contractor, based in Wakefield, [Massachusetts] would split the cost of refunds. Clark is the first school to try the guarantee.

"Let's say that a student selects a roast beef meal, but finds that the roast beef has been over-cooked," Foley said. "The student should bring it to the attention of a food-services manager, who will then offer the student one of the other meals—perhaps fish or pizza—being served that day. If that doesn't work, then food services will offer to fix the student, say, a stir-fried meal or a special omelet. If all that doesn't satisfy the student, we'll refund the price of the meal. All we ask is that the student consider reasonable alternatives."

Everyone who lives in the dorms at Clark University must buy a meal plan, and 1,350 of the 2,200 undergraduates eat in the school dining halls.

> Worcester Telegram & Gazette
> *January 13, 1990*
> *Lynne Tolman*

What were the results of Clark University's money-back guarantee? Between January 1990 and the spring of 1991, according to Director of Dining Services Joe Kraskouskas, 28 refunds were credited against a couple of hundred thousand meals. After an initial flurry of activity, approximately one student every two weeks requests a food-service manager to adjust the menu. Daka has gone so far as to make a steak for a student who was dissatisfied, or cook a pasta meal on the spot, or grill a sandwich. "We have always been willing to make a substitution if a student was unhappy," Kraskouskas emphasized. "The difference is that now the students know it."

The guarantee is only part of Daka's concern with promoting customer satisfaction. In addition, managers sit in each of the two dining halls every Wednesday as part of a proactive management program. Students are invited to discuss menus, make requests, or voice complaints. Whether the exchange concerns bananas in the jello or the number of salad bowls available, a record of conversations is kept and a list of questions and answers is posted every week for the information of other diners. Daka also made a decision to have a complete vegetarian menu available starting April 12, 1991, in response to student requests.

Kraskouskas feels like the guarantee has done what it intended. "We put our money where our mouth is," he stated. "Students know they have recourse when they are dissatisfied." The guarantee was designed to be user friendly. A dining guide with the guarantee on the back is given to every student at the beginning of the semester. A point of sale banner restates the guarantee, and Plexiglas table tents on every table tell students how to get an alternative meal or a refund. "It has made us more accountable," he said.

Axiom #71 *When designing a program to increase customer satisfaction, a guarantee is just the beginning. A good design also includes plans to actively solicit customers' opinions.*

72 Documentation
Backing Opinion with Facts

*T*he housekeeping staff knew there was a problem. The phone was constantly ringing off the hook, especially during the evening shift. Worse, there was only one phone, and routine tasks were neglected as one associate after another rushed across the room to answer it promptly. Clearly something had to be done.

The situation at the Chicago Downtown Marriott may not have been that unusual, but the solution was. When housekeepers brought the problem to the attention of their manager, they were asked what they would like to do to solve it. Their first instinct was to ask for the installation of another phone, located across the room from the first. It would save steps, it was relatively inexpensive, and it could be done quickly. Management concurred.

During the discussion on exactly where to install the new line, one associate offered the opinion that a second phone wouldn't be necessary if people would just stop calling about irons and ironing boards. That opinion was immediately popular, which led the manager to ask for a best guess as to what percentage of calls were on that topic. There was general agreement that at least two-thirds of the calls fit into that category.

Here was an opportunity to solve the larger problem. A plan of attack was devised. Housekeepers began to sort calls by topic and keep track with tally marks. They soon found out that their best guess was wrong. Almost 90 percent of the calls were requests for irons and ironing boards.

Armed with this documentation, the manager approached the executive committee with the suggestion that each room be equipped with these items. The executive committee agreed that it sounded like a good idea but demurred at the expense.

Housekeeping followed up by doing research and determined that $20,000 would do the job. They also found an item in the new budget for $20,000 for black-and-white television sets for guest bathrooms. A look at the telephone log revealed that housekeeping had never had a request for a television set for the bathroom.

Once again, their manager approached the executive committee. The final decision was that it is better to give guests what they want, not what you think they want. Funds were transferred, each guest room was equipped with an ironing board and an iron, and housekeeping got some (relative) peace and quiet.

* * *

Encouraged by the results in housekeeping, Michelle began to keep a record of how she spent time when she was on duty at the front desk of the Chicago Downtown Marriott. She knew she had too much dead time. She also knew she was too busy at her own desk when she was not taking her turn on the front desk.

By multiplying her salary times the number of hours spent waiting for something to happen, she discovered that the dollar figure covered the cost of a personal computer. She used her documentation to approach management. Her argument was that she was well aware of the priorities of the front desk—guests came first—but wasting time was demoralizing for her and hardly in the best interests of the Marriott.

Again, management concurred. A personal computer was installed. Michelle was able to control her workflow, avoid boredom, and take on new duties at her other desk.

Axiom #72 *When you can document your solution with hard numbers, you are more likely to get what you want.*

73 *Effectiveness*
China in Russia: A Study in Quality (out of) Control

*I*magine a manufacturer that delays the quality control check until the last possible moment. Imagine a retailer that uses a procedure that requires three separate interactions for each purchase. Imagine, in short, buying china in Russia.

In the summer of 1990, a pair of American quality professionals, on tour in the USSR as part of a People-to-People exchange of information about computer quality assurance, audit, and data security, walked into a major department store in Moscow. A line of over 50 people on the first floor led to the chinaware counter, an indication that a shipment of china had just arrived. There was one pattern available. China was stacked in piles on the floor behind the counter, plates in one pile, cups in another, saucers and bowls in still others. Three clerks dealt with the crowd.

The procedure for buying chinaware was a lengthy one. First, a customer stood in line for 20 to 30 minutes. Once at the counter, she (most of the customers were women) would tell the clerk how many plates/cups/bowls/saucers she wanted ... in today's pattern. The clerk would calculate the cost on her abacus (clerks in this store were all women) and hand the customer a slip of paper.

The customer then got in another line, one that led to the only clerk empowered to take money for several counters of merchandise. This clerk was located in a small cage in the middle of the floor and had a cash register. After another 30-minute wait, money was exchanged, and the customer received a piece of paper confirming payment.

The customer was then required to get back in the first line to endure another long wait—although some customers waved their receipts and were allowed to jump the queue.

Finally, the customer presented the receipt to a clerk who filled the order from the stacks behind her on the floor. If, for instance, the customer had ordered eight plates, the clerk bent to count eight plates and lifted them onto the counter. Then picking up the plates one at a time, she did a quality control check. Using a long, thin wand (about the size of a chopstick), she struck each plate and listened to the resultant tone. If the "ding" sounded true, the plate was stacked to the right. If a "dong" clanked, the plate was discarded.

When the order was filled, the china was bundled up in paper and corded. The customer then put the china in her "perhaps" bag, the ubiquitous shopping accouterment carried by every woman, every day, on the off chance that something might be worth buying.

The Russians who took part in this transaction—or to whom this transaction was described—did not appear to find it disturbing. One Russian was of the opinion that the final check was necessary because of the number of items broken in transit.

The three-step purchase procedure is common throughout the Soviet Union. Russians tell visitors that it is not wise to trust every clerk to take money. Petty theft is rife. And besides, "We've always done it that way." Oddly enough, this system is not found in the Beriozka stores where foreign guests buy goods for hard currency. There it is possible to browse amid the merchandise, make a selection, and pay on the way out.

To the American observers it appeared that the china manufacturer chose the least efficient and most expensive method for assuring that only quality products made it into the consumers' hands, expending maximum funds before trashing poor products. As for spending well over an hour to buy an item, any item, if the Beriozka stores can solve the problem, why not the large department stores?

Axiom #**73** *Common sense isn't so common. Whenever there is an observable waste of time, money, and physical resources, there has to be a better way. True quality requires both effectiveness and efficiency. It may be easier to make excuses for the current state of affairs, but it won't solve the problem.*

74 *Experience*

Experienced Employees Are the Best Judges of Quality

*T*he North Pacific Paper Corporation (NORPAC) mill, a joint venture between Weyerhaeuser Company of Tacoma, Washington, and Tokyo-based Jujo Paper Company produces over 1250 tons of high-quality newsprint (the paper used for the printing of newspapers) per day. It is an operation marked by two distinguishing characteristics: a belief in the abilities of its employees and a knowledge of customer expectations.

The guidelines for inspecting the massive rolls of paper were developed by a joint management-nonmanagement team. While they appear vague to the outsider, experienced employees making sophisticated judgments insure their effectiveness:

- Corrugation—Little Tolerance (judgment may require input from supervisor or dry end operator)
- Slack Start @ Core—Very Little Tolerance
- Slack Start @ Splice—No Tolerance
- Protruding Paper in Roll—Very Little Tolerance (Sand-Off)
- Wrinkles—No Tolerance
- Cuts—No Tolerance
- Scales—Slight Tolerance
- Bad Splice—No Tolerance—Flap ⅛″ Max.
- Dishing—2mm Export, 3⁄16″ Domestic
- Splices—3 Max., Over 1″ Apart, None in top 1″, Domestic
- Splices—Export—1 Splice, Can Not Be Within Top 20mm

Rolls of newsprint that are judged by the employees to measure up to the "Export" standards are shipped to Japan; lesser rolls are sold to virtually every leading newspaper in the United States.

The Harden Furniture Company is located in McConnellsville, New York. Their quality process is rooted in the belief that their employees take pride in their slogan "Fine furniture from generation to generation."

Every department of the company has quality standards that were developed by quality teams within those departments and which are displayed prominently within the department work area. The management of Harden admits that employees established tougher standards than management would have, had the choice been theirs. Yet, while being unquestionably high, the standards are also spelled out in such a way as to assume that they are being read, and followed, by adults.

The Sewing Department Quality Standards contain language that respects the individual's judgment. Note particularly the reference to "earliest or most economical stage":

1. All sewing operations must be performed as outlined in the sewing procedures book or according to the foreman's instructions.
2. *Accuracy is essential:*
   - All seams must be straight.
   - All seam allowances must be maintained.
   - Top and bottom corners of cushion bands must be lined up.
   - Read work orders and tickets carefully—watch for special instructions.
3. All defects must be removed at the earliest or most economical stage, at the foreman's discretion.
4. Teamwork and cooperation are essential to a quality job in the Sewing Department.

This same respect for employees' expertise is reflected in the Roughmill Quality Standards:

1. Cut for maximum efficiency.
2. *Accuracy is essential:*
   - Cuts must be square.
   - No short boards.
   - No narrow panels.
   - Check set ups periodically for accuracy.
   - Calibrate your rule weekly.
3. *Maintain lumber grades:*
   - *A Grade*—No defects permitted.
   - *C Grade*—Structurally Sound—Cosmetic Defects Only
4. No excessively warped boards in panels.

5. No thin boards in panels finishing ⅞″ + 1⅛″

6. Count pieces in the job and mark back of jacket.

The Hardware Department Quality Standards assumes that employees will have no difficulty deciding what is "proper":

1. *Handle with care*—finished pieces are fragile.
2. *Accuracy is essential:*
   - Read tickets *carefully*—check for special instructions.
   - Proper installation and alignment of hardware is critical.
   - Proper alignment and fitting of tops and bases is critical.
   - Proper operation of drawers, doors, locks, pull out shelves, and lighting fixtures is critical.
   - Remove all skids and clean bases completely.
   - All pieces must be thoroughly cleaned before wrapping.
   - Be sure that all necessary parts (literature, keys, shelf supports, etc.) are properly secured in piece [*sic*].
3. *Remember*, the next person to see this piece is the customer: *check it carefully!*

Andrew Clark, the Director of Safety and Quality at Harden, says of the Harden employees, "Their knowledge of the product is a resource that cannot be overlooked when you are trying to upgrade your product."

It is an attitude that is the hallmark of organizations committed to the idea of continuous improvement.

Axiom #**74** *It's far easier to say to outsiders, "Oh, yes, we believe that our employees are our greatest asset," than it is to say to employees, "You know what is right. Set your standards and do it." Trusting employees—believing that they are adults who want the company to succeed and then acting on that belief—is rarely better demonstrated than when dealing with questions of measurement. Given the opportunity and support, employees will set and maintain rigorous standards.*

75 Feedback

Prescription for Quality: Large Doses of Information

*I*ntermountain Health Care (IHC) of Salt Lake City, Utah, is a national leader in the study and practice of quality in the health care field. Their QUE (Quality, Utilization, and Efficiency) model focuses on "units of care." Units of care correspond to individual items in a detailed patient bill, such as a single dose of a drug, one minute in a surgical suite, or one day on an acute care nursing floor.

Physician utilization patterns, as expressed in numbers of specific units of care, can be analyzed—once a balanced group of patients is determined. A "balanced group of patients" is one in which patients entered medical care with equal severity of illness and exited with equal outcomes (complications and medical results).

A QUE study tracks a specific ailment and its treatment by specific doctors at specific hospitals for a period of time and accumulates data as to units of care expended. The data is carefully "blinded" so that no one in authority can use the data to single out individual doctors or hospitals whose expenditures of units of care is above average.

Feedback is presented to the doctors in two forms. Each doctor receives a confidential report of his or her own performance along with the data for the entire group. Each can then see where he or she is in the group and take part in subsequent discussions and comparisons.

No further directive action is taken by the researchers or administrators. An assumption is made that "most individuals— 85 to 90 percent—pursue high-quality work as a personal value; it is only necessary to supply adequate data and training to achieve high-quality results. This may be even more true in clinical medicine, which tends to attract those with a personal commitment to serve."

Results bear out this assumption. Repeatedly in QUE studies (and in similar data-gathering and delivery efforts at other medical facilities), the doctors involved in the studies "self-corrected" with no further external motivation or direction. Within a very short period of time, the data points converged toward the "good" end of the particular scale. For example, in one study conducted by the IHC researchers, the mean length of stay in the hospital following a particular operation (transurethal prostatectomy) decreased nearly 36 percent (from 4.40 days to 2.53 days) in just nine months following the distribution of data to the physicians at the hospital.

In another study, the operation researched was total hip joint replacement, excluding fractures. This operation was chosen for study both because of its importance (without a hip joint replacement, many patients are consigned to being permanently bedridden) and because of its cost. The doctors in the IHC system perform between 700 and 800 hip joint replacement operations in a typical year.

As can be seen in the accompanying chart, on page 187, the average length of stay for a patient undergoing the operation prior to the QUE study was 10 days (the 15-day average recorded for January 1988 was a statistical "spike"). The first results of the study were distributed to the physicians in August 1988. An immediate drop in the average length of stay can be seen on the chart.

The continuing decline in the average length of stay was also the result of a related, concurrent project. Inspired by their initial success, teams of physicians formed to study specific aspects of the total operation. A major factor in increased cost and increased time for the operation was found to be the variety of hip joint replacement kits available on the market.

Barring any specific guidance, the various doctors had each developed favorites. Since so many different "brands" were being

DRG 209* MEDICARE LENGTH OF STAY
Avg Length of Stay and 2 Std Dev Lines

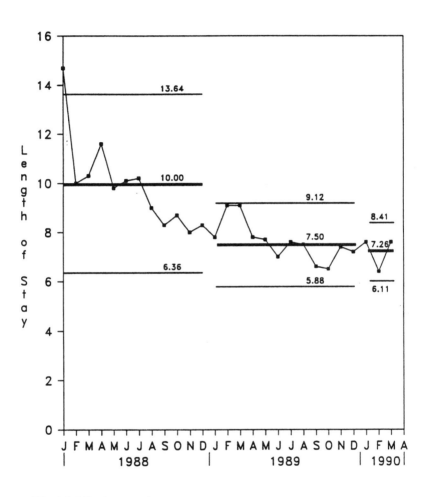

* Hip Joint Replacement

used, the hospitals did not keep any in inventory but rather bought each one on a special-order basis as needed. A further impact of this proliferation of types was that a doctor might find himself or herself with the "wrong" kit for a particular operation, or with a mixed kit.

A team of surgeons studied the available options and settled on one particular kit as the best option for 80 percent of the operations and two others as appropriate for the remaining 20 percent. With that decision, the hospital began to order in bulk, realizing a substantial savings, plus the doctors and operating room staffs became familiar with the peculiarities of each type of hip joint replacement kit—which resulted in both smoother, quicker operations and a further reduction in the average length of stay.

Also of note in the accompanying chart is the fact that the variation from month to month decreased with the passage of time. Dr. Brent James, who directs the effort at IHC, credits this to the fact that the doctors begin to align their behavior with the best performer in each category. Rather than settle for a comfortable "average," everyone moves toward the leaders.

This last point may be the biggest single benefit of the entire process. IHC's use of measurement allows all of its doctors to learn the best practices available for each technique.

Axiom #**75** *Improvements can be achieved by putting the appropriate data in the right hands and then getting out of the way.*

76 *Function*
Doing the Right Things
vs.
Doing Things Right

A quality process addresses two separate, intertwined questions: "Are we doing the right things?" and "Are we doing things right?" It is, after all, possible to do the wrong things well, just as it is possible to do the right things badly. For success, an organization needs to do the right things and do them well.

Several tools, each with a specialized vocabulary, have been developed to answer the need to identify the right things to do. Value Analysis and Service Blueprints are two of them. A brief look at each illustrates how they are used to manage and modify a company's operations.

In 1947, Lawrence Miles, then a purchasing agent for General Electric, developed the concept of Value Analysis. His method shifted the focus from the physical aspects of a product to its function. This shift enabled him to determine whether the sequence of operations used to design and produce the product, taken as a whole, consumed the fewest resources while preserving the desired outcome. This tool has since been used to analyze products, processes, departments, and myriad other complex functions looking for ways to simplify, eliminate, combine, rearrange, substitute for, standardize, or otherwise modify inputs in the interests of reducing the cost of the outcome.

Value Analysis has seven main steps: preparation, information, analysis, creativity, evaluation, recommendation, and implementation. The first step requires selecting a project and setting aside time for an exchange of information between people who contribute to its outcome. In the case of product design or process analysis, the workshop would be cross-functional. The next step is to gather relevant data.

A clear, if nontraditional, example of Value Analysis shows how it could be used to restructure a department within an organization. These first two steps are satisfied by planning a series of three-to-four-hour meetings, typically taking place twice a week for six to eight weeks, and involving the decision-makers of the department undergoing Value Analysis. The goal of these workshops is to produce a list of recommendations for implementation.

The analytical stage requires participants to describe the department's function in two words, one verb, one noun. Activities within the department are also described in two-word phrases. Activities are then divided into primary ones—those that contribute directly to the essential function of the department, and secondary ones—those that make the accomplishment of the essential function possible while not contributing directly to it. These can be represented in a functional wiring diagram. Those tasks which are neither primary nor secondary are clear candidates for elimination.

The remaining meetings of the workshop cover the creative phase, devoted to deciding on alternative ways to improve the execution of each task; the evaluation phase, prioritizing viable choices by taking into account the value of the task in the eyes of customer(s); and recommendations. Before recommendations can be approved, measurements to track progress toward the implementation of the agreed-upon decisions are developed.

Service Blueprints grew out of the conviction of G. Lynn Shostack, chairman and CEO of Joyce International, Inc., that service was so fundamentally different from manufacturing that there had to be a new way to talk about it and visualize it. First presented in 1984, Shostack begins by conceptualizing service as an integrated system with three basic elements: process (tasks and activities), means (people and goods), and evidence (what the consumer experiences). She postulates that a change in any element will almost always impact the other two, and that an ongoing service design function composed of these three elements is a necessity.

Her methodology for the design function is Service Blueprints. Blueprinting is what the name implies. It is the graphic representation of how a particular service system functions. Lines of communication as well as the sequence of value-added tasks are represented. Beginning with an overview blueprint, subsidiary blueprints and micro-level blueprints are developed. Shostack's position is that a good design embraces the smallest details.

This information can be used to manage service systems in a number of ways. By actually diagramming the flow of information and resources, serious anomalies and flat-out weaknesses—possible fail points—can be uncovered. Every step, activity, and event can be quantified by the cost of the time it takes to perform. Actual service can be compared to this model. Opportunities for improving quality and profitability are uncovered. Within the organization, blueprints can be used as a basis for communication and training for employees. They are especially helpful as a tool to raise the level of consciousness regarding what the customer does and does not see.

With either Value Analysis or Service Blueprints, a management team is frequently well advised to invite (hire) an outside facilitator to lead them through the exercise. This may be someone "outside" the department but within the company, if the company is large enough to carry a person with Value Analysis or Service Blueprints skills on its payroll. More commonly, the facilitator is Service Blueprints from outside the organization. In any case, facilitators need to be chosen with care. Discussion of the right thing to do can become intense. In addition to experience, knowledge of the techniques in question and their application, and familiarity with theories on quality and quality processes, the ability to lead discussions without getting hopelessly bogged down (or without terminally antagonizing the participants) is of prime consideration.

Both Value Analysis and Service Blueprints do have a potential for misuse. They must not become a straightjacket. Respect for the judgment of individual employees is essential to quality. Specific steps must be designed in such a way that employees feel free to innovate, to solve problems, and to perform their jobs without the fear that they will be criticized.

Axiom #**76** *While every employee makes decisions every day on whether or not tasks are being performed correctly ("Are we doing things right?"), management has the additional responsibility of deciding what tasks need to be performed ("Are we doing the right things?"). Value Analysis and Service Blueprints are two tools available to assist in this task.*

77 *Goals*
Is Perfection a Reasonable Goal?

*I*n fields that call for innovation and creativity, zero defects is not only impossible, it is totally inappropriate. Exploration of new possibilities, by its very nature, produces far more defects than perfect solutions. Life, however, has many repetitive actions, and there is a valid argument to be made for zero defects as a goal in these cases.

The recognition of the problems inherent in even a 1 percent error rate are obvious in a wide array of situations. A contributor to a Dear Abby column, Don McNeill of Sepulveda, California, once pointed out that if only a 1 percent error is allowed, the following conditions would prevail:

- At least 200,000 incorrect drug prescriptions each year.
- More than 30,000 newborn babies accidentally dropped by doctors and/or nurses each year.
- Unsafe drinking water almost four days each year.
- No electricity, water, or heat for about 15 minutes each day.

- No telephone service or television transmission for nearly 15 minutes each day.
- Newspapers not delivered four times each year.

The *Total Quality Management Guide*, a Department of Defense manual, uses the illustration that if 99 percent accuracy is considered sufficient, there will be "two short or long landings at most major airports each day."

In point of fact, everyone expects to be the *beneficiary* of perfection all the time. (Imagine if your heart decided to take a break for 5 percent of each day; it would mean a "work stoppage" of 72 minutes out of every 24 hours.) But *benefiting from* perfection and *producing* perfection are two very different issues.

Is perfection a realistic request of an employee, especially one whose actions do not carry life-and-death implications? Employees often produce 100 percent satisfactory results off the job, even if they do not recognize it as such.

Suppose, for instance, an employee works for a company in a medium-sized city, where there may be well over 250,000 residences (houses, apartments, mobile homes, etc.) within a reasonable driving distance of his or her place of employment. At the end of a hard day's work, when he or she gets into the car and heads home, that employee appears to have a 1 in 250,000 chance of finding the correct residence on the first try.

Looked at as a mathematical problem, the odds are staggering. When leaving the parking lot, the employee is immediately faced with a three-way decision: Should she or he go straight, to the left, or to the right? Similar decisions await at every intersection. (This analogy also illustrates the relatively disastrous impact of errors made early in a process, as compared to those made later. To miss the first turn could land the driver in the next state, even if he or she follows all the rest of the steps accurately. Blow just the last turn and it might be possible to park the car and walk home.)

Yet the overwhelming majority of employees accurately and efficiently make their way home every day—even if they have to make an in-course correction due to special circumstances, such as closed bridges or traffic accidents in the road ahead. They expect to do so and would find it unacceptable not to do so.

What contributes to this ability to produce perfection? The seemingly unsolvable navigation problem is handled adroitly because the employee chooses the final goal, understands the value of reaching it, and has control over the sequence of decisions necessary to reach it. In short, the employee "owns" the process. These conditions can be repeated in a corporate setting.

At the outset of World War II, American Army paratroopers suffered from what can accurately be called a "quality problem." Some of their parachutes weren't opening.

Not many were defective. In fact, if totals were kept and the number of nonopening parachutes were considered in comparison to the number that did open properly during a time span of sufficient length, it could be shown that the number of failures was "well within variance." Variance is, however, a tough concept to explain to someone who is hurtling toward the ground.

The solution was to go to the parachute packers and—in today's vocabulary—involve them in what amounted to a tightly focused quality process by saying, in essence, "Congratulations! From now on, every now and again, on a random basis, you get to jump . . . using the last parachute you packed."

The percentage of correctly packed parachutes immediately jumped to 100 percent and stayed there throughout the war.

Axiom #77 *Abigail Van Buren puts it succinctly, "I say, always strive for perfection but allow for human error." George Fisher, president and CEO of Motorola, a 1988 Malcolm Baldrige National Quality Award winner, would agree, but he might add "but not too much of it." He talks about 6 sigma quality—a goal of only 3.4 errors per million. He hopes to be talking about errors per billion by 1992. That's pretty close to perfection.*

78 Guidelines
Malcolm Baldrige
National Quality Award

*N*ational quality awards are a relatively new phenomenon. The Deming Prize in Japan was first established in 1950. Since then, Great Britain (1984), the United States (1987), Australia (1988), France (1989), Mexico (1990), and Canada (1991) have also established national quality awards, and the European Foundation of Quality Management is currently in the process of defining a quality award, conceivably for the European Economic Community.

The United States Malcolm Baldrige National Quality Award is named for a former secretary of commerce (1981–1987). It is a joint effort of government and private enterprise managed by the National Institute of Standards and Technology, United States Department of Commerce, and administered by the American Society for Quality Control, a professional society. An endowment to permanently fund the Award program has been established through the Foundation for the Malcolm Baldrige National Quality Award, a private sector endeavor created for that purpose. Applications are reviewed without funding from the United States government.

The first presentation of awards was by President Ronald Reagan on November 14, 1988, to three winners, two in the manufacturing category and one in small business. The first recipients were Motorola Inc., the Commercial Nuclear Fuel Division of Westinghouse Electric Corporation, and Globe Metallurgical Inc., respectively. There were two manufacturing winners in 1989, Milliken & Company and Xerox Business Products and Systems. Federal Express Corporation was the first winner in the service category in 1990, accompanied by Cadillac Motor Car Division and IBM Rochester in manufacturing, and Wallace Co., Inc. (also service) in small business.

Initially, the award grew out of efforts by private enterprise. Beginning in 1984, representatives of the American Productivity Center (which later became the American Productivity and Quality Center) and several diverse companies, including an automobile manufacturer, a food processor, an insurance company, an airplane manufacturer, and a financial service company, met in Washington, D.C., to discuss creating a national quality award. Over the next three years, their efforts were joined by the American Society for Quality Control and a major electrical power company. Momentum for Congressional legislation resulted in the Malcolm Baldrige National Quality Improvement Act of 1987, signed into law on August 20 of that year.

National quality awards can serve a number of purposes. The *1991 Application Guidelines* sets out the goals of the Baldrige Award:

> The Malcolm Baldrige National Quality Award is an annual Award to recognize U.S. companies which excel in quality achievement and quality management.
>   The Award promotes:
>
> - awareness of quality as an increasingly important element in competitiveness,
> - understanding of the requirements for quality excellence, and
> - sharing of information on successful quality strategies and on the benefits derived from implementation of these strategies.

Applying for the award is a rigorous procedure consisting of submitting a 75-page-maximum report (50 pages maximum for a small business) answering questions in seven categories: Leadership, Information and Analysis, Strategic Quality Planning, Human Resource Utilization, Quality Assurance of Products and Services, Quality Results, and Customer Satisfaction. The scoring is heavily weighted to make Customer Satisfaction the most important determinate of quality. Each applicant receives a written report that provides individual feedback in these areas.

A Board of Examiners evaluates the applications; at least four

Examiners score each application. The Board is comprised of more than 200 quality experts who have completed a preparation course based on the examination items, the scoring criteria, and the examination process. Once applications are evaluated, companies judged by consensus review to have superlative quality receive a two- or three-day site visit from a team of at least five Examiners. The purpose of this site visit is to verify information contained in the application.

The site visits are followed by a final review by a Panel of Judges empowered to give out six awards, or fewer, depending upon whether or not there are any applicants who meet the Award's standards. Judges combine scores from the written application with observations from the site visits to assess overall strengths and areas for improvement. Two Awards may be given in each of three separate categories: manufacturing, service, and small business. (Small business is defined as those businesses with fewer than 500 employees.) Government agencies, nonprofit organizations, and professional organizations and trade associations are not eligible to compete.

Not surprisingly, the number of applicants for the Award has been small—66 in 1988, only 40 in 1989, rising to 97 in 1990 and 104 in 1991. Preparation of a written report amounts to a full-quality audit of a company and requires both quantitative data and trend data spanning up to five years. The number of requests for application guidelines, however, has risen sharply from 12,000 in 1988 to over 45,000 in 1989, 180,000 in 1990, and 250,000 in 1991. This testifies to the use of the application itself as an educational tool.

What makes the *Application Guidelines* so useful is that it is both universal and flexible. It is universal in that it clearly identifies the ultimate aim of all quality improvement—customer satisfaction—and the underlying issues which all companies must face—leadership, information, process, participation, and measurement. It is flexible in that no one approach is required of all companies. Instead, the 1991 application has 99 areas to address, organized into 7 categories and 32 examination items. Scoring is based on three types of evaluation: approach, deployment, and results.

The guidelines have encouraged interest in quality awards in a way that the Deming Prize failed to do, but the United States Malcolm Baldrige National Quality Award is not without controversy. Much discussion has been devoted to the relative weight given each of the categories. There also has been concern that the guidelines tend to reward the kinds of processes and measurements found in manufacturing quality control at the expense of less traditional approaches found in service companies. If such a manufacturing bias exists, it becomes less apparent with successive rewritings of the guidelines. The guidelines themselves are the object of yearly review and continuous improvement.

In the words of President George Bush, "The improvement of quality in products and the improvement of quality in service—these are national priorities as never before." The Malcolm Baldrige National Quality Award encourages this improvement.

1991 EXAMINATION CATEGORIES AND ITEMS

1991 Examination Categories/Items	*Maximum Points*	
1.0 Leadership		**100**
1.1 Senior Executive Leadership	40	
1.2 Quality Values	15	
1.3 Management for Quality	25	
1.4 Public Responsibility	20	
2.0 Information and Analysis		**70**
2.1 Scope and Management of Quality Data and Information	20	
2.2 Competitive Comparisons and Benchmarks	30	
2.3 Analysis of Quality Data and Information	20	
3.0 Strategic Quality Planning		**60**
3.1 Strategic Quality Planning Process	35	
3.2 Quality Goals and Plans	25	

1991 Examination Categories/Items	Maximum Points	
4.0 Human Resource Utilization		**150**
4.1 Human Resource Management	20	
4.2 Employee Involvement	40	
4.3 Quality Education and Training	40	
4.4 Employee Recognition and Performance Measurement	25	
4.5 Employee Well-Being and Morale	25	
5.0 Quality Assurance of Products and Services		**140**
5.1 Design and Introduction of Quality Products and Services	35	
5.2 Process Quality Control	20	
5.3 Continuous Improvement of Processes	20	
5.4 Quality Assessment	15	
5.5 Documentation	10	
5.6 Business Process and Support Service Quality	20	
5.7 Supplier Quality	20	
6.0 Quality Results		**180**
6.1 Product and Service Quality Results	90	
6.2 Business Process, Operational and Support Service Quality Results	50	
6.3 Supplier Quality Results	40	
7.0 Customer Satisfaction		**300**
7.1 Determining Customer Requirements and Expectations	30	
7.2 Customer Relationship Management	50	
7.3 Customer Service Standards	20	
7.4 Commitment to Customers	15	
7.5 Complaint Resolution for Quality Improvement	25	
7.6 Determining Customer Satisfaction	20	
7.7 Customer Satisfaction Results	70	
7.8 Customer Satisfaction Comparison	70	
Total Points		**1000**

Axiom #**78** *When wondering what to measure to improve quality, help is available. The* Application Guidelines for the Malcolm Baldrige National Quality Award *provide a universal and flexible tool for evaluating quality efforts.*

79 Integration
From Cop to Coach—A New Role for Quality Control Specialists

*M*ost organizations have long had some individual—or some small beleaguered group—on their payroll with a job title that includes either the word "quality" or "productivity," often followed by either "control" or "assurance." These individuals traditionally play an adversarial role, consisting of 1) trying to catch others' mistakes after those mistakes have already been made, or 2) advising other employees on how to change their on-the-job behavior in the interests of greater speed and efficiency—usually unsolicited advice.

The 1980s brought a whole new wave of job titles that included the word "quality" ("productivity" has fallen into disuse), but now it is a noun rather than an adjective—as in "Vice President for Total Quality." This individual is usually tasked with encouraging employees to be responsible for their own quality, to set up their own quality checks, and to modify their own jobs as anomalies are uncovered.

Where do the old quality/productivity professionals fit into one of these new "total quality" processes? Very near its heart. One of the first tasks of any newly appointed vice-president (or director or manager or whatever) of quality (or total quality) is to identify the quality control and quality assurance people already on the payroll and to work with them to identify and define a new status.

This new role might start with a change in title. "Quality Analyst" accurately reflects the abilities of these individuals. These men and women, up to now the keepers of the flame of quality, know things about the company and how the component pieces of the organization fit together that nobody else knows. They know where the problems are, what processes are most likely to fail, and who can fix things.

As analysts, their new job is to put their skills at the disposal of other employees as coaches, teachers, trainers, and motivators. This is a move away from the authoritarian one-way information conduits of old and a move toward becoming willing and knowledgeable resources.

Both the new analysts and the other employees will have to adjust to the change. At first, the old joke about "We're from the IRS and we're here to help" will most likely find its way into conversations around the company.

It is possible to structure the situation within the company so that other employees will *invite* the quality analysts to inspect their work and offer advice. Once a team of employees decides on a change in their work area and implements it, the next procedural step toward receiving credit for the improvement can be a visit from a quality analyst.

In this scenario, a quality analyst becomes the source of good news ("The change you decided on works") rather than the bearer of bad news ("You have to change the way you do things"). By having an analyst certify a quality idea after it has already been implemented by a team, the company still retains the benefits of the analyst's expertise. Calculations of productivity gains are verified; good-faith mistakes can be corrected before they become deeply ingrained habits. The analyst can suggest further enhancements and act as idea-pollinator, spreading information about ideas applicable to more than one department.

The goal is to train every employee to draw on the analysts' acknowledged skills as productivity specialists, in the same way that a management team draws on their expertise in the design of new products and services. The potential for analysts to permanently impact the way business is conducted in the organization is far greater in this new role than it ever was in their original role as pseudo-police. At the same time, the company retains the invaluable corporate memory held by this team.

Correct use of the quality control, quality assurance, and productivity professionals already on the payroll can save a company from having to reinvent a number of wheels as the idea of quality is elevated from being the singular concern of a small band of renegades to being a mainstream priority.

Axiom #**79** *The individuals traditionally responsible for quality control are not made obsolete by a quality process. Their skills are an integral part of any quality effort. When quality control specialists share their skills with a wide range of employees, they become an invaluable asset to the company.*

80 *Intention*
A Saga of Sales Sapped by Legal Lingo

*T*he first-time author was as proud of his new book as any new parent would be of his first offspring. Like so many authors before him, he was certain that *everyone* would want to buy a copy. To aid in that effort, the publishing company provided him with order forms to distribute whenever he spoke on topics covered in the volume. The idea was to enable audiences to acquire the book as easily as possible.

Even though the author's speaking engagements steadily increased, very few people used the book order forms. It was very, very disappointing. It took awhile for the author to track down the reason. An embarrassing 18 months later, he took the time to read the flyer carefully.

Right above the line that read "Payment enclosed," was the sentence, "If shipment is not made within 90 days, check is refunded." When he called the publishing company to find out why the "If we don't get around to it in three months, we'll send your money back" line was included, the response was, "The lawyers require it." When he suggested that it might be wiser to improve the turnaround time for book orders, the company assured him that he didn't understand the difficulties.

The author then met the owner of a local book store that prided itself on its customer service. "Let me make up some order forms for you," offered Lawrence J. Abramoff, the owner of Tatnuck Bookseller and Sons in Worcester, Massachusetts.

The new form looked almost exactly like the previous one. There were only two changes. In place of the "We'll get to it one of these days, maybe" line, the order form now said, "Shipping by UPS within 2 days." And the address to which the customer's money should be sent had changed.

Tatnuck sold over 3000 copies of the book out of the one book store. The customers were happy, the book store owner was happy, and the author was delirious with joy.

Unfortunately, this is not a perfect cautionary tale. The publishers were also happy—even though they had to share the profits.

Axiom #80 *While not offered as a guarantee, the legal tag in the first form is tantamount to a guarantee of nonservice. Implicitly, up-to-90 days is the* published measure *for what the company considers acceptable response time. It informs the reader that the customer cannot hold the publisher responsible for timely service. The company intended to protect itself in an unusual case; the result was to discourage the customer in virtually every case.*

81 Interpretation
Let Logic Prevail

During the Vietnam War, the United States and South Vietnam established several programs aimed at convincing enemy soldiers to switch sides. One program, which enjoyed enough success to be resurrected for use in the Gulf War, was the air-dropped "Chieu Hoi" (or "Open Arms") pamphlet program.

The idea was simple enough. Pamphlets were printed that explained in some detail what benefits awaited any North Vietnamese or Viet Cong soldier who voluntarily gave himself up to the American or South Vietnamese forces. Everything from food to money to freedom from military trials was promised.

After the first drop of the pamphlets, some Communist soldiers did, in fact, come out of the jungles carrying the pamphlets and claiming the promised rewards.

A State Department analyst on the scene immediately saw the potential. First he divided the number of pamphlets dropped by the number of defectors to determine a pamphlet-per-defector factor. Then he went looking for an estimate of how many troops would have to defect from the Communist forces in order to render them militarily ineffective.

His proposed plan, once he had that number, was to multiply it times the PPD (pamphlet-per-defector) factor to find out how many pamphlets needed to be dropped to bring a swift end to the war.

Logic prevailed.

Axiom #81 *A short course in logic is an excellent accompaniment to measurement.*

82 Nonconformance
Taking a Cost of Quality Survey

Cost of Quality (COQ) is more a concept than an exact science, and a not particularly tidy or aptly named concept at that. More accurately referred to as the Cost of Nonconformance or the Cost of Non-Quality, COQ is an attempt to express in one number— as a percentage of gross sales—the dollar figure attached both to making sure that things are done right (prevention) and to recovering when things are done wrong (detection and correction).

Determining the COQ can be difficult; there is not even universal agreement as to what primary elements make up the total cost. While almost everyone agrees on prevention, detection, and correction, some individuals and organizations urge the inclusion of a "correction-failure" category in order to get a complete picture. The difference between "correction" and "correction-failure," they posit, is determined by the paying customer's reaction. If the customer is lost to the organization because of the failure, then a reasonable estimate of the dollar loss to the company should be included in the COQ calculations as correction-failure.

Computing a supportable dollar figure for COQ is tricky. As with so many things that go into an overall quality effort, the determination of a COQ figure is even more difficult in a service organization, or the service elements of a manufacturing organization, than it is in a manufacturing concern. All of the elements of COQ are inexact; correction-failure is the least precise. Moreover, it has been argued that computing COQ is an intellectual exercise, at best, and that there are more effective ways to make the same point.

Take the amount of waste generated by doing things wrong. While in a service company evidence of failure is not readily evident to the casual observer, it is in a manufacturing organization. A manufacturing CEO who wants to impress upon all employees that there is too much waste—either rework or scrap—can have all of it saved for a period of time and dumped in front of the main entrance of the plant one morning. Dramatic, yes, and potentially effective. If it were possible to do the same in a service company, the calculation of COQ would be a less useful tool. As it is, no such heart-gripping demonstration is possible in service. A large pile of paper (assuming someone really could determine exactly which sheets of paper represented waste and which didn't) just doesn't get the juices flowing.

Having made the case for not computing COQ, it may seem perverse to urge organizations to do so. Nonetheless, there are excellent reasons for making the effort. A COQ survey can act as a catalyst for all employees to assess how their time is being spent and, when administered periodically, enable the organization as a whole to measure progress in controlling costs resulting from nonconformance. By identifying where such costs are high, a COQ survey can help determine where to concentrate resources to support improvement efforts.

While admitting that COQ is inexact, COQ can play an important role in quality education and awareness. There will always be a cost of quality, even if it is only a prevention cost. Prevention includes the costs associated with training and the establishment of procedures and purchase of machinery whose purpose it is to ensure that mistakes do not occur. This cost will never go to zero. In fact, as an organization's quality process matures, an increasing percentage of its COQ expenditures will shift into prevention.

Employees who understand the concept of COQ will be sensitive to this shift. Prevention is money well spent. Experience has proven repeatedly that, no matter what the industry, an ounce of prevention is indeed worth at least a pound of cure.

In order for employees to understand the implications of COQ, several things have to occur. Employees must be involved in computing the COQ figure. It is true that a single committee of top and middle managers could settle on a defendable number as their company's COQ after a series of debates, augmented by hard data and a large dollop of experience. But, to what end? To announce to the employees at large that, "Our cost of quality is 36 percent of our gross sales" would produce a figure close to what is believed to be the American average for a service organization. But what would it mean to the individual employee?

Employees who analyze how their time is spent benefit in two ways. They are more aware of the link between time and money, and they spot opportunities for using time more productively.

What follows is a suggested methodology for a COQ survey. Make sure the survey form contains the basic COQ definitions and information, information on "why we are doing this," plus examples of possible actions that could fall into each of the categories: prevention, detection, correction, and, if desired, correction-failure. The form should also ask for each employee's job level—not a name, not a department. The job level is necessary to final calculations since it is important to know if the 100 hours spent correcting errors is costing the company $8 an hour or $100 an hour.

Begin by dividing the entire company into "reporting units." If a 100 percent employee involvement quality process is in place, then the Quality Teams are a natural choice. In any other environment, some other way to split up the payroll must be determined (by department, for example, or by task).

Follow with orientation training for all employees. What is a COQ survey? Why is it being taken? How do you compute COQ? If we define rework as undesirable, what happens to the employee whose job is rework? Employees must be reassured that no one's job is in danger. It would also be a good idea to reassure them that there is no "correct COQ" and that top management knows that the dollar figure attached to COQ is likely to be high. Maybe even embarrassingly high.

After the general awareness/education program, reporting

unit leaders can meet to discuss the survey form and its use. The next step is to have each employee fill out a form giving his or her best estimate of how much time is spent in each of the first three categories in an average week or month—and, if desired, how much money (in the form of missed sales) should be included in the fourth category. These numbers are estimates. The assumption is that a whole series of honest best estimates will tally up to a reasonably accurate number. It is more important that the methodology used be consistent from year to year than it is that the procedure be absolutely, theoretically perfect.

Reporting unit leaders turn the completed forms in to a central point. At the central point, the data are totaled. The first COQ survey becomes the company's baseline. COQ surveys should be repeated periodically, for example, annually or biannually. The determination of data by employees will identify areas to be improved; the totals—by being relatively accurate—will indicate what progress is being made from year to year.

COQ information can be used to assess how much of the company's funds—and profits—are being chewed up by doing things wrong. What should happen, of course, is that the relative amount of time being devoted to preventing, detecting, and correcting problems should go down. This is true even if the absolute figure remains stubbornly static. If the dollar figure associated with COQ remains the same during a period when gross sales double, then the percentage represented by COQ is cut in half.

Axiom #**82** *A Cost of Quality survey can educate employees as to the importance of prevention versus detection and correction. Survey results can also be a benchmark for progress and a source of ideas for improvement.*

83 *Precision*

Measureless Chocolate Chip Cookies

Yields a Passel of Coin-Sized Cookies

Preheat oven until hot.

Cream:
   A dollop of butter

Add gradually and beat until creamy:
   A handful of brown sugar
   A fistful of white sugar

Beat in:
   Egg
   A splash of vanilla

Sift and stir in:
   A heap of sifted all-purpose flour plus a smidgen more
   A soupçon of salt
   Scant baking soda

Stir in:
   A modicum of chopped nut meats
   A plentitude of semisweet chocolate chips

Drop the batter from an average-sized spoon, spaced well apart, on a greased cookie sheet. Bake until done.

Axiom #**83** *There are occasions when precise measurements are necessary to assure a favorable outcome. There is no more reason to be concerned about taking these measurements on the job than there is in the home. Anyone who can follow a recipe, understand sports statistics, or read a map can use measurement on the job.*

84 *Prevention*
An Ambulance Down
in the Valley

*E*ntertainer and environmentalist John Denver reads *An Ambulance Down in the Valley* (credited to "Anonymous") at many of his concerts:

> 'Twas a dangerous cliff as they freely confessed,
> Though to walk near its edge was so pleasant.
> But over its edge had slipped a Duke,
> And it fooled many a peasant.
>
> The people said something would have to be done,
> But their projects did not at all tally.
> Some said, "Put a fence around the edge of the cliff,"
> Others, "An ambulance down in the valley."
>
> The lament of the crowd was profound and loud,
> As their hearts overflowed with pity;
> But the ambulance carried the cry of the day,
> As it spread to the neighboring cities.
> So a collection was made to accumulate aid,
> And dwellers in highway and alley,
> Gave dollars and cents not to furnish a fence
> But an ambulance down in the valley.
>
> "For the cliff is all right if you're careful," they said,
> "And if folks ever slip and are falling;
> It's not the slipping and falling that hurts them so
>   much,
> As the shock down below when they're stopping."
>
> And so for the years as these mishaps occurred,
> Quick forth would the rescuers sally,
> To pick up the victims who fell from the cliff
> With the ambulance down in the valley.

Said one in his plea, "It's a marvel to me
That you'd give so much greater attention,
To repairing results than to curing the cause;
Why you'd much better aim at prevention.
For the mischief, of course, should be stopped at its
    source;
Come friends and neighbors, let us rally!
It makes far better sense to rely on a fence,
Than an ambulance down in the valley."

"He's wrong in his head," the majority said.
"He would end all our earnest endeavors.
He's the kind of a man that would shirk his
    responsible work,
But we will support it forever.
Aren't we picking up all just as fast as they fall,
And giving them care liberally?
Why, a superfluous fence is of no consequence,
If the ambulance works in the valley."

Now this story seems queer as I've given it here,
But things oft occur which are stranger.
More humane we assert to repair the hurt,
Then the plan of removing the danger.
The best possible course would be to safeguard the
    source,
And to attend to things rationally.
Yes, build up the fence and let us dispense,
With this ambulance down in the valley.

Axiom #**84** *Shifting the Cost of Quality into prevention isn't always easy, even when it pays off in dollars and cents. Preserving the status quo has its own appeal. For example, if a production facility begins making everything right the first time, what happens to the customer service department?*

85 *Proactive*

Police Story: The Case of the Cop and His Customers

*A*uburn, Massachusetts, is a town of just over 15,000 citizens, located in the central part of the state, adjacent to the city of Worcester. Late in January 1991, 300 of those citizens received a survey in the mail with the following cover letter:[2]

Dear Auburn Resident,

Since becoming Auburn's Police Chief in January of 1988, I have continually strived to serve the needs of the community to the best of my abilities. It is often a difficult task, however, to define with any certainty what those needs may be. This is especially true when there are very diverse interests which need to be addressed, as there are in the Town of Auburn. For example, many issues which members of the local business community feel should be police priorities may differ markedly from those which local residents view as being of prime importance. In addition, frequently the feedback a police administrator receives from the community may be limited or come from only a small number of the various groups he or she is trying to serve.

Consequently, the Auburn Police Department is conducting a citizen survey in an attempt to identify more clearly those issues which are most important to the community, as well as to determine the perceived quality level of police service in the Town of Auburn.

In an attempt to remain as objective as possible, the survey has been developed by a person who is not a member of the police department or an employee of the Town of Auburn. This individual, who is conducting the survey as a part of his post-graduate studies in Criminal Justice at Anna Maria College, will also be responsible for collecting and evaluating the resulting data. It is important that respondents do not sign or otherwise identify themselves on the survey form so that all responses remain anonymous. The results of the study will be made public and a copy will be on file at the Auburn Public Library for review.

It is the hope of the entire police department that through this survey we will be able to better serve the Auburn community. We ask that you be as frank and open as possible when answering the questions on the accompanying form and that it be returned no later than February 15, 1991 in the enclosed, stamped and addressed envelope. This survey is only the beginning of what will be an on-going attempt by the Auburn Police Department to actively involve the people it serves in developing the overall police mission.

Thank you for both your time and your interest.

Respectfully yours,

Ronald W. Miller
Chief of Police

Miller had been looking for a proactive way to gain a better understanding of the needs and perceptions of the residents of Auburn. His prior experience on a police force in a city 10 times Auburn's size led him to believe that Auburn had a different set of expectations for its police force.

Andrew Boyd was a former policeman who had become an eighth-grade teacher. He was working on his master's degree in criminal justice at Anna Maria College when he became a student in a class taught by Chief Miller. He was looking for an indepen-dent study project.

The two agreed that a survey would achieve both their goals. After initial discussions, Boyd designed a 45-question survey and had it reviewed by both Miller and a former nun who now teaches measurement and evaluation courses at Anna Maria. The result was a slightly altered 43-question survey. One of the changes, for instance, was the removal of a question about the level of funding received by the police department. Inclusion of the question, Miller felt, might lead to the impression that the "secret agenda" of the survey was to get ammunition for a budget battle with the town council.

The 300 citizens who received the surveys were chosen from

two groups. The first 150 were chosen at random from the town voter listings. The second 150 were chosen at random from the police department's computers. The people listed in the police department's computers were all those people who had ever had contact with the Auburn police for one reason or another—from calling to complain about a barking dog to being arrested. The only qualifier added to the selection of the second group was that they had to be residents of Auburn.

The return rate from the first group was just short of 40 percent; from the second group, just above 33 percent. To the surprise of the surveyor, there did not appear to be any statistical difference in the answers from the two groups.

In fact, the answers were also consistent across virtually all age groups. One minor difference was that the oldest citizens appeared to be a bit less satisfied with the overall service than any of the younger groups.

The returned surveys were rich in marginalia. One respondent went to some length to complain about a ticket that he had received three years previously for a "rolling stop." In response to the question "How would you rate the overall performance of the last Auburn police officer you had direct contact with?" he marked "Superior."

Miller intends to involve his police officers—who have voiced support for the survey from the outset—in the decisions about what changes need to be made in police procedures. If, for instance, the assessment by the residents of a particular neighborhood is that their streets are not patrolled frequently enough, it will be up to the officers responsible for that area to decide how to change the schedule and/or the perception.

A second problem to be resolved by the policemen is the faithfulness of follow-up calls. A frequent complaint is that policemen don't get back to the original caller after resolution of a problem—be it a noisy party or a possible crime in progress. The objective reality may well be that the information is used, that action is taken, and that everyone is very busy, but the perception is that the caller is being ignored. Politely, perhaps, but ignored nonetheless. The 24 police officers (13 have degrees in criminal justice, at least two others have college degrees) and 4 dispatchers will decide how to change procedures so that perception and reality can more closely match.

The survey, the minimal cost of which came out of the department's training budget, is to be repeated on a periodic basis in the coming years.

Chief Miller reports one early result. Many people have stopped him on the streets to tell him how pleased they are that he asked.

Axiom #**85** *Even public servants have customers. The same measurement tools used in the private sector to find out what the customer wants can be used in the public sector for the same purpose.*

86 Process
Measurement Methodology at Mutual

In the spring of 1991, Mutual of Omaha Companies, Omaha, Nebraska, launched a 100 percent involvement Quality Improvement Process (QIP). As part of the preparation for the process, a packet of training materials addressing the issue of measurement was distributed. The cover letter explained the use of measurement in relationship to the QIP:[3]

> The measurement of nonconformance is an important step in the Quality Improvement Process (QIP). Measurement used in the QIP differs from some of our traditional measurement concepts. Measurement is used in the QIP as a tool that allows us to understand what is happening so we can communicate to others and implement corrective action.

Because of the importance of QIP measurement, we all need to have a common understanding of it. The attached Measurement Policy summarizes some of the key points discussed at the QIP Training sessions for the measurement step. This Policy can be used as a reference to help you successfully complete the measurement step, as well as insure consistent application throughout the Companies. More detailed information on determining what and how to measure is included in your training materials.

As you implement measurements in your areas, keep in mind that all work is a process, most problems are caused by the process and not individuals, and that measurement is simply a tool we use to implement preventive actions and arrive at solutions to problems.

As a guide to use in identifying what and how to measure, the package of materials included a "Measurement Worksheet" consisting of 10 questions to be addressed when considering the initiation of any measurements.

MEASUREMENT IDENTIFICATION WORKSHEET

1. What process is to be measured?
We should choose a process that we know or suspect is not conforming to requirements, or one that offers an opportunity for significant improvement. Ask yourself, is there a problem with the particular process? Is there a process that is meeting requirements, but can be done in a more effective or efficient manner? Review of our process model worksheets and calculations of price of nonconformance can help us determine what to measure.

2. Which part of the process? Which requirement(s)?
It is important to choose specific requirements to measure against. The employees in the work unit should make the choice based upon their knowledge of the outputs, inputs, and the process itself.

3. Why was this part/requirement chosen?
We choose measurements that, based upon our knowledge, will most accurately reflect the performance of the process. We should ask the questions: Will improvement in this area save money or time? Is there frustration or waste because the requirement is not met? Will this measurement accurately focus attention on a problem or potential problem?

4. How will the data be collected?

The accuracy of counts is critical. The best approach for accumulating counts of nonconformance is to design a check sheet that captures the data as the nonconformances are observed. [Sample check sheets were included as part of the materials.]

5. Who will be responsible for data collection?

Someone must be made responsible for measurements and recording them according to an established procedure. Requirements of this task must be clearly understood by those given this responsibility. Normally, the individuals actively involved in the process should be responsible for collecting the data.

6. What kind of chart will be used and how will it be labeled?

Charts displaying nonconformances are to be used by work units, areas, and departments. These charts should normally be displayed so they are visible to all those who need to know this information. In most situations, a run chart will be the best method for communicating measurement results. Standard run charts are available and can be requested through Purchasing. [A sample run chart and instructions for obtaining and completing the run chart were included.]

7. Who will be responsible for recording information?

Normally, someone involved in the process should be responsible for recording the information on the charts.

8. Who routinely needs to be aware of the data?

For measurement to direct improvement, the results must be seen by those involved in the improvement efforts. These would normally include the people operating the process, management, and others such as suppliers, customers, or anyone who could help to improve the process.

9. How will the information be communicated to those identified above?

Charts should be displayed in a central location within a work unit, area, or department where they are visible to visitors and employees actively involved in the process. Copies of the charts can be sent to other individuals who need the information to affect improvement.

10. Who should be responsible for taking action based upon the information?

Normally, if it is within the ability of those involved in the process, they should assume responsibility for actions to improve based upon the information measured. If it is beyond that area's capability to affect improvement, they must take responsibility for communicating the information to someone who can make the necessary changes.

In support of all the pronouncements and guidelines is the Mutual of Omaha Companies Quality Improvement Process Measurement Policy:

Purpose

By charting and measuring nonconformances to requirements, we can better determine areas that need improvement, evaluate, and plan corrective action.

Policy

—The Quality Improvement Process (QIP) will measure work *processes, inputs*, and *outputs*. The purpose of QIP is not to measure individuals. QIP measurement charts will not be used in developing performance appraisals.

—All employees will be given training, materials, and assistance to help them understand the measurement process.

—Each work group will measure the work processes, inputs or outputs that do not conform to requirements. The employees within each work group will determine what and how to measure.

—Only outputs that do not conform to requirements will be *displayed*. Inputs measured from outside the work group will *not* be *displayed*.

—Work groups throughout the Companies will use the same measurement displays and charts, to ensure consistency and readability.

—Measurement charts will be displayed in a prominent location within each department, easily seen by employees and visitors.

—Measurement charts will be updated on a regular basis.

—Success stories will be recognized and shared among work areas.

Axiom #86 *When everyone in the company becomes a quality manager, everyone must be aware of the pitfalls of measurement. Mutual of Omaha has avoided the four reasons why quality managers fail, as given by Dr. Joseph Juran:*

- *Preoccupied with conformance to specifications rather than focusing on fitness for use.*
- *More concerned with appropriateness of their methods and procedures than with what is right for their business.*
- *Become in-grown, oblivious to the world around them . . . major concern is meeting the goals of the quality department with little regard for what is happening in other areas.*
- *Unfamiliar with, or cannot cope with, corporate culture.*

87 Progress
The Mechanics of Tracking a Quality Process

A quality process is an ordered, if not always orderly, business process. Keeping track of a quality process in a businesslike manner enables an organization to record progress, exchange ideas, check to see if an improvement fits into the overall scheme of things, standardize calculations of time and money saved, and assure recognition of achievements.

In 1984, Paul Revere Insurance Group, Worcester, Massachusetts, designed a computer program to report the results of its Quality Has Value process. Dubbed the Quality Team Tracking Program, QTTP was a conceptually simple file program available at virtually every computer terminal in the company. The company divided its employees into teams empowered to make changes in their areas of responsibility and report the results through the computer. The file was formed by linking individual team files.

A team file consisted of a series of formatted screens, each designed to hold one idea. (Some other companies' versions use two screens per idea.) Aside from the identification information, the most important elements were the description of the idea and the status of the idea.

When an idea was first entered in the file, the team status was normally set to "1," indicating that the team was working on it. If a delay developed during efforts to implement the idea, the team could change the status to a "2." A "3" indicated that the idea, on second thought, was not going to be pursued, while a "4" meant the idea had been implemented.

By using the status code from the QTTP screens, Paul Revere's Quality Team Central (QTC) could see what the teams had been doing. Members of QTC were productivity analysts with skills in work measurement and work simplification projects. At least once a week, QTC got a listing of all "4's" (implemented ideas) from the QTTP. The appropriate team leaders were contacted and appointments were made. The purpose of an appointment was to certify the idea.

Certification had three parts. The aptness of the idea was considered, the implementation of the idea was checked for impact on any other area of the company, and calculations of savings were verified. Once the idea was certified, the team leader changed the status code to a "5," and the team was given credit toward recognition.

The simplicity of the program worked in its favor. Without QTTP, Quality Team Central would have been swamped in paper. With the QTTP, the entire logging and certification process was reduced to two loose-leaf binders and periodic computer printouts. At the other end of the process, because there was no paper to be generated, team leaders felt much more inclined to proceed with "small" ideas—the ones that look unimpressive to someone three or four levels up the corporate wiring diagram but are key to establishing a habit of quality.

The QTTP was also an important communications link. Although a team leader could only change his or her own team's file, any team leader could examine the entire QTTP file. After the initial excitement, team leaders tended to look at their own file, the files of teams with similar responsibilities (stealing or duplicating ideas was encouraged), the file of the team their boss was on, and the file of the top management team. Knowing that the top management team—at Paul Revere known as "The Big

Guys"—was active was a powerful message to the rest of the company.

Paul Revere's QTTP made it not only possible but easy for any team of employees to quietly benchmark themselves against the best in the company in a setting where nobody's success was at anyone else's expense.

In a less enlightened company in the Dark Ages of 1988, a consultant explained to a seminar of top executives the use of a computer program to track team efforts to improve quality.

"We couldn't do that," one vice-president stated.

"Why not?" replied the puzzled consultant.

"Because I would check to see if my subordinates' teams had as many ideas as those of other executives—and if they didn't, I'd pressure them," the vice-president explained patiently. Other executives present, including the president of the company, agreed.

"But that's not the intent," argued the consultant. "The intent of the tracking system is to keep track of the progress, be sure that no good-faith mistakes are being made, and say thank you on a timely basis."

"That's not how we'd use it."

"But you can *choose* how you use it."

"Not here. Here if you give me numbers, I use them to find out who's messing up."

"Let me get this straight," said the astounded consultant. "Are you saying, 'Stop me before I kill again'?"

"Yes," was the unanimous answer.

Proving again that it is possible to misuse even the most benign system.

Axiom #**87** *Measurements taken in the course of a quality process can be used to track progress. They can also be used to assign blame. In an organization that combines measurement with sound leadership and participation principles there is less potential for abuse.*

88 *Quantitativeness*
How Do I Love Thee?
Let Me Track the Data

*B*illy was in love. Or at least he thought he was. Whenever he was with Maggie, he felt happy and they seemed to keep finding new things to do, new ways to please each other.

He told his friend George. George was not convinced. "How do you know that you are in love?" he asked. "How do you know that Maggie really cares for you? Where is your documentation? What quantitative data do you have? What makes you think it will last?"

Billy hadn't really thought of his actions—or his feelings—in that light. He felt a little silly when he realized that he was treating his relationship with Maggie as if it were the first time in history that a young man had fallen in love with and wanted to please a young lady. He had thought of Maggie and himself as unique.

George's questions woke him up. It wasn't enough to feel special; there were methods to be used to assure that the relationship progressed, processes to be employed to assure a long-lasting, happy ending.

He didn't see Maggie as often the next few weeks. With George's help, he was busy studying, concentrating on learning the right, proven way to retain a girl's affection. Maggie thought Billy was mad at her for some reason because he didn't explain his absence.

When he had finished the training course that he and George had defined (mostly a combination of reading about measurement systems and viewing videotapes of classic, romantic movies), he was able to approach his time with Maggie on a far more intelligent, well-planned, better-defined basis.

After each date, he carefully recorded what he had done and

what Maggie's reactions had appeared to be. As a continuing baseline, he periodically took his own pulse during the course of each date.

He cross-referenced time, total mileage recorded during a date, money spent, meals eaten, and the number of slow and fast dances with his impression of how much Maggie appeared to enjoy the evening and to further accept him into her life.

It confused him that the more he tracked the data and the more he tried to repeat exactly what had seemed to elicit a positive response on previous dates, the lower his "reaction of Maggie on a scale of 1 to 10" scores became.

He was also a bit bothered because when he compared Maggie point-by-point to his "ideal partner" (a theoretical person he had defined during his training period), she didn't measure up as well as he would have expected. He knew he loved her . . . at least, he thought he knew he loved her, but the numbers just weren't there.

He was having trouble pinpointing the difficulty. Was he doing the right thing? And was he doing it right? Or was it Maggie? With George's help, he produced more and more charts and defined more and more measures. He found himself cutting his dates short so that he could get home and update his database.

Of course, he never exactly told Maggie what he was doing. For one thing, he knew she didn't understand (or like) George. She called him "George the Geek." Besides, to let her in on the study would have unavoidably biased the data.

He did ask her, with increasing frequency, if she was enjoying herself and if she would like someday to repeat a certain activity. Occasionally, he would even ask her to rate her happiness at a given moment on a scale of 1 to 10.

When Maggie left him, it did not come as a big surprise to Billy. The numbers had been slipping for some weeks.

But he was still sad.

Axiom #88 *Just because a measurement can be taken doesn't mean it should be. Just because a calculation can be made doesn't mean that it must be made or that it makes sense.*

89 Reaction
The Impact of Variability

Quality is about how organizations react to variability. While manufacturing operations are focused on identifying, measuring, and bringing product variability under control, service quality efforts are primarily concerned with identifying, measuring, and adjusting to variability resulting from interactions with customers. Simply put, the goal is to reduce variability in manufacturing quality; the goal is to be prepared for variability with service quality.

This defines a basic difference in the use and relative weight given various types of measurements in service organizations (including the service components of manufacturing companies) and in manufacturing operations. Consider the use of Statistical Process Control (SPC) and survey techniques and their impact on employee behavior in the two settings.

Dr. Juran's definition of quality, "Fitness for use," is concise and accurate in a manufacturing environment. Manufactured items most often do physically fit into, or with, some other manufactured item. This is true of component goods being assembled inside an organization or of final products used in conjunction with other items by the customer.

Because it is possible to control the precision with which an item is manufactured, most manufacturing decisions are based on objective and/or physical measurement. Is it the right length? Width? Weight? Is the difference from piece to piece within limits? Is it displaying a normal distribution in its variance—or should something be changed to make sure the process stays in control? These questions lend themselves to SPC charting.

The measurements taken in the course of a manufacturing quality effort quite often are particularized down to specific machines, with operators given the authority to make adjustments in response to the data. What adjustments to make are admittedly subjective judgments based on experience, but they tend to be physical adjustments, objectively repeatable.

Services, however, must "fit" within a customer's mental expectations, making Juran's definition somewhat nebulous. It is impossible to "prove" to someone that they have just had a wonderful experience using objective criteria if he or she doesn't believe it. It doesn't matter to what extent the service, in measurable fact, fulfills some promised criteria.

It is impossible to keep customer expectations "in control"— which is the mistake service companies make when they try to duplicate manufacturing's approach to quality. An SPC chart in a service setting can be useful as a diagnostic tool indicating when a situation is out of control, but unlike manufacturing, it yields few clues as to remedies.

Major misapprehensions occur when service organizations try too hard to make their measurements "objective" and "straightforward." This can lead to futile exercises, such as trying to chart how many times an airline stewardess smiles each hour. The attempt to use a physical measurement (smiles per hour per stewardess) to get an accurate reading on a subjective outcome (were the passengers satisfied enough to seek out this airline for their next trip?) is clumsy at best.

A service organization has no real option but to concentrate on reacting to changes in customer expectations, a requirement that is equally true whether the customer is internal or external to the organization. Efforts to evaluate service quality call for subjective and/or attitudinal measurements.

Meeting service expectations requires a degree of flexibility rarely found in manufacturing. Customer expectations tend to change more slowly in manufacturing (imagine a hotel customer waiting patiently for "next year's model"?) and to be relatively well articulated. Manufacturing has physical limits as to how fast processes can be altered, and customers for the most part understand that, but changes in service are often asked for and expected with the speed of thought.

As a result, numerous and frequent surveys of customers have become a major tool in service organizations. Service quality surveys are wide ranging in their use and in the techniques employed. "How am I doing?" cards and carefully staged, scientifically conducted focus groups both fall within the definition of efforts to keep up with external customer expectations. Within an organization, everything from informal questions such as "Is this what you want?" to formal survey instruments meets the need to define internal customer expectations. All surveys yield fuzzier results than physical gauges, but they are a proven indicator of trends in customer satisfaction. Service employees can react to survey results to ameliorate a situation just as manufacturing employees react to SPC results if they are given the authority to do so.

Note that taking physical measurements does not free the manufacturer from periodically polling customers any more than keeping in close touch with customers frees the service provider from the need to monitor the physical properties of services provided. Wherever variability occurs, it must be analyzed and managed.

Axiom #**89** *Variability is unavoidable. Using measurement tools aids employees in lessening its impact.*

90 Recovery
Converting Customer Dissatisfaction into Customer Loyalty

"**D**on't worry about your broken arm, my dear, because when it heals, the bone will be even stronger than it was." Thus have thousands of young children been comforted by their mothers over the years.

Now there is growing evidence that the it-will-be-stronger-once-it-has-healed bromide may be true with customer-provider relationships. Researchers have begun to develop data indicating that a customer who has been dissatisfied in some way, but who is subsequently the recipient of a good "recovery" strategy, will feel more loyal toward an organization than one who has always received good services or products.

The leading writer/original thinker on the topic of "customer recovery" is Ron Zemke. Also prominent in this new field of research is John Goodman and his TARP (Technical Assistance Research Programs) organization. The research being done by Zemke, Goodman, and others is basically a form of measurement that assesses customers' reactions once they have actually purchased a product or service. Such information can be used to recover from individual problems, but it also closes the loop begun by an organization's R&D department, yielding information on how to modify these same (and future) products and services to prevent problems.

Zemke proposes that an organization have a "planned service recovery," which he defines as "a thought-out, planned process for returning aggrieved customers to a state of satisfaction with the organization after a service or product has failed to live up to expectations."

He cites TARP research that indicates how such a plan can salvage a situation:

> First, swift and effective service recovery enhances customers' perception of the quality of products or services they have already purchased.
>
> Second, it enhances their perception of the organization's competence.
>
> Finally, good recovery enhances the perceived quality and value of other products and services the organization offers.

Customers who do complain should be cherished by the offending organization because they are 1) the best source of ideas for improvements and 2) rare. What do customers want when things go wrong? Zemke's research indicates that the customer would be happy with four things:

1. To receive an apology for the fact that the customer is inconvenienced.
2. To be offered a "fair fix" for the problem.
3. To be treated in a way that suggests the company cares about the problem, about fixing the problem and about the customer's inconvenience.
4. To be offered some value-added atonement for the inconvenience.

What they emphatically do *not* want is to be treated like a nuisance—even if the problem was caused by their actions. Zemke states that, "Consistently good recovery is achieved only through a set of systems, operations and actions that are painstakingly planned, constantly refined and carefully executed."

It may seem odd to plan for things to go wrong, but "TARP's general finding is that product production may contribute to only one-third of all customer dissatisfaction. This means that two-thirds of all dissatisfaction is not caused by the traditional targets of QA (quality assurance) analysis. If QA is to make the most of its ability to minimize customer problems, it must expand the arena in which it has traditionally operated."

QA can have an impact by becoming more proactive in finding out how customers misuse products and then producing countermeasures—more complete directions, better training for sales personnel, or customer education. Statistically, it appears that only 4 to 10 percent of dissatisfied customers ever actually complain to the organization about a service or product. The other 90 to 96 percent do complain but not *to* the organization that might be able to do something about it. Rather, they complain *about* the organization—to anyone else who will listen. In fact, many customers make it a minicrusade of sorts.

In view of these numbers, aggressive tactics are necessary. Even if the problems are caused in part or in whole by the customers, it remains their money, and it remains their decision as to where to spend next month's paycheck.

Some of the more innovative companies have devised ways to entice potentially unhappy customers to talk to them before dissatisfaction occurs. Armstrong World Industries discovered that the low maintenance, "no-wax" finishes on its floorings were failing with alarming frequency—because the customers weren't following directions on how to maintain them. So they put an "800" number on the top side of the floor itself.

Customers had to call the 800 number to learn how to take the number off the flooring. While the Armstrong people had the customers on the phone, they were able to explain proper maintenance to them. Armstrong estimates that the few dollars each 800 call cost them saved the company a potential $12,000 in revenue per customer over the customer's average period of loyalty.

One of the key goals of a service-recovery strategy is to insure that customers never even consider the competition. No matter what Company A's research might say about the inferior quality of Competitor B's service or product, some of A's customers will—illogically or otherwise—prefer B *if they give it a chance*. This is particularly possible if they feel as if they have been mistreated by A. Had AT&T taken Sprint and MCI seriously right from the start, those two upstarts would not be the serious contenders they are today. Any business person who says, "Ah, let them try the other guy; they'll be back!" is a candidate for membership in the Edsel Club.

Axiom #**90** *According to Ron Zemke, "The true test of an organization's commitment to service quality isn't the stylishness of the pledge it makes in its marketing literature; it's in the way the company responds when things go wrong for the customer." The same is true with product quality.*

91 *Relevance*
Measurement Without Merit

As of January 1990, it is illegal to let a phone ring more than 10 times in a state office in California. State Senator William Lockyer introduced the legislation as an inspiration "to motivate bureaucrats to provide improved service." There is no funding included for adding any personnel to the state payroll. There are no penalties defined for violators.

Ringing phones are clearly one of the three major frustrations of modern life, accompanied by not being able to get anything but a busy signal when trying to make a call and by being put on hold—seemingly forever.

Despite the new law, the Tax Department still handles only 67 percent of its calls during an average day, the Department of Motor Vehicles still puts customers on hold for up to 30 minutes, and the secretary of state says it still takes five to six days to complete a call for information about a company incorporated in California.

—Statistics from
Wall Street Journal
January 9, 1990

Quality also matters in the Soviet Union, but the Russians have a different way of achieving it. A Ukrainian court recently sentenced three female factory managers to two years in a labor camp and fined them $14,000 for producing poor quality clothes at a government factory, according to the Tass news agency. The harsh punishment represented the first application of a new Ukrainian law on quality control standards, an issue close to the heart of Soviet boss Mikhail Gorbachev. Just to make sure offenders don't miss the point, the three women, after serving their terms, will be forced to forfeit 20 percent of their future salaries to the state for an indefinite period.

—The Boston Globe
December 23, 1986

Calvin and Hobbes   by Bill Watterson

Bill Watterson
Worcester Telegram & Gazette[4]

Axiom #**91** *Measurements used incorrectly can be ludicrous. Even worse, taking irrelevant measurements is destructive to morale and can produce unforeseen negative results.*

92 Reward
"Close Enough for Government Work" No Longer Cuts It for Government Work

*T*he first Quality Improvement Prototype for the President's Productivity Improvement Program was awarded to the Naval Aviation Depot at Cherry Point, North Carolina, in mid-1988. "A prototype organization demonstrates an extraordinary commitment to quality improvement, focuses attention on satisfying its customers, and establishes high standards of quality, timeliness and efficiency," said Office of Management and Budget Director James C. Miller, III, in announcing the award.

The depot, which employs 3100 civilians, is one of six naval aviation depots (the only one directed by the Marines) that furnish worldwide aeronautical maintenance and logistics support for all branches of the U.S. Armed Forces and other government activities.

The award was earned through the depot's implementation of a total quality process and a Gain Sharing program. In the case of the former, it has proven to be one of the best in the government; in the case of the latter, it was the first federal facility to implement such a plan.

The commanding officer, Colonel Jerald Gartman, set about establishing a "quality culture" shortly after assuming command in early 1986. There were some initial difficulties. In fact, Gartman has since said that, "Some people thought that I'd have the shortest tenure of any commander here."

By June 1990, however, he was able to report that, "The depot has increased productivity 73 percent in the grind-plate-grind process, reduced engine test failures by 90 percent, and reduced inspection rejects of helicopter rotor hub repairs by 80 percent." Another example of increased productivity was the application of statistical process control to the process of coating jet engine blades—an operation that is performed hundreds of thousands of times a year. The reject rate fell from a "traditional" level of 50 percent to less than three-fourths of 1 percent.

No small operation, the depot is an industrial complex made up of more than 90 buildings totaling approximately one-and-a-half million square feet. Its functions—and opportunities for improvement—are, naturally, diverse. Some of the examples cited in a May 11, 1990, "Special Quarterly Edition" of *NADEP NEWS* included:

Message errors

Process: Secretaries and clerical personnel type messages utilizing the Joint Message Form, DD Form 173, which are then forwarded to the Communications-Electronics Department of the Air Station for electronic transmission. Errors and defects are detected during the initial visual screen and by the Optical Character Reading (OCR). The facility was experiencing a 14.46 percent error rate.

Analysis: There are 24 types of errors possible on a message. A Pareto Analysis was conducted to identify the largest source of errors. It clearly identified Type 4 errors (addressee unidentifiable or invalid, unauthorized plain language address) as the source of over 42 percent of the errors. Continued study showed that most of these errors were purely typographical, e.g., the transposition of letters in NAVAVNLOGCEN.

Process Improvement: All sections of the depot were screened to identify commonly used addresses. They were entered into a file within the central word processing system. Personnel may now electronically "cut and paste" correctly spelled addresses into their messages. This file is maintained by the Office Services Division (110). Also, a "Help" screen was designed and placed in the word processor to help minimize the other 23 types of errors. The message error rate is being tracked by Pareto Analysis, and efforts are still being made to reduce the percentage of errors.

Productivity Gain:
Error Rate Prior to Improvement: 14.46 percent
Error Rate After Improvement: 8.49 percent
Productivity Improvement: 41 percent (322 less defects per year)

Combustion chambers repaired

Process: The T76 Engine Combustion Chamber was routed for rework of a crack which exceeded the limits in the overhaul instructions.

Analysis: The location of the crack was evaluated. It was determined that it was not located in a critical area and that a weld repair would not adversely affect safety or serviceability.

Process Improvement: The combustion chambers are now repaired and returned to service rather than being scrapped.

Productivity Gain:
Material Cost for Former Workloads: $6940 Per Unit
Labor Cost for Future Workloads: $16 Per Unit
Productivity Improvement Per Unit: 99.7 percent

New design improvement

Process: The test equipment used to test the C-130 Aircraft Gearbox Actuators had been adapted for use from other test equipment.

Analysis: The test equipment was difficult to operate and test readings were questionable.

Process Improvement: An improved test console was designed and built in accordance with the manual specifications and approved by the Product Support Directorate (50). This new tester saves manhours and assures accurate testing, thus producing a higher quality product.

Productivity Improvement:

Labor Cost for Former Workloads: $6.48
Labor Cost for Future Workloads: $3.24
Productivity Improvement Per Unit: 50 percent

Additional examples of gains in quality and productivity through the use of statistical process control and teamwork abound, with savings ranging from a few pennies per repetition of a particular action (e.g., reducing the cost of cleaning components prior to sandblasting from $13.30 to $13.18) to savings that run into the tens of thousands of dollars per year. Standard repair and maintenance on one type of aircraft dropped as much as $55,000 from January 1986 to September 1987. Both large and small gains are rewarded.

The Gain Sharing program implemented at Cherry Point was a first for employees drawing a United States government paycheck. *Gain Sharing in a Total Quality Environment* coauthored by Colonel Gartman and John S.W. Fargher, Jr., the head of the business office at the depot, is a paper stating, "PGS [profit gains sharing] is a means to motivate artisans and managers alike to focus on working harder and smarter. Along with increased physical effort, managers and artisans alike must work together to fully implement the strategic plan, use SPC/TQM (Statistical Process Control/Total Quality Management) as a tool for continuous process improvement, and measure results in increased quality and productivity and reduced costs."

The Gain Sharing program applies to all civilian employees on the payroll on the last day of the last full pay period of a quarter (with minor exceptions). Once the amount of the "pool" of saved money is determined (through a very well-publicized formula), it is split 50-50 between the base and the employees. The employees' half is then divided by the number of people eligible, and everybody, regardless of position on the hierarchy/payroll, receives the same size check. For the second quarter of fiscal year 1990, the payout was $169 (after taxes) per employee, bringing the total paid out to the employees since the beginning of the program to approximately $5,500,000.

In addition to all the statistical data, Gartman and Fargher have formalized the management philosophy in a paper on *Employee Participation and Self Management*. It includes passages that indicate why measurement works:

> The concepts of TQM are not difficult and the SPC tools are fairly readily learned and applied. Some workers may initially resist involvement if they view TQM as a threat to their job or a management "trick" to extract more work. This resistance should soon disappear as they see their responsibilities, authority, and accountability expand; become more involved in operational and ultimately policy issues; see a reduction of administrative controls and quality reviews; and sense not only participation, involvement, and empowerment, but also ownership of specific processes. These work force teams ultimately are involved in the overall company processes and in effect become the "company team" ...
>
> As the depot artisans and support personnel have participated and become proficient in the application of SPC, communications barriers have been reduced and pride in the quality of the product has increased. Through the application of the TQM philosophy, the role of the artisan is changing toward self-management. The changes noted are not only that of process and quality improvement but also increased individual efforts. Managers are assuming the role of facilitators, teachers, and coordinators, establishing priorities and goals but not specifically directing the work. The framework established through the previously mentioned productivity and quality improvement efforts provides the philosophy and tools for both the artisan and supervisor to assume these new roles.

Axiom #92 *With award-winning quality, leadership and participation are indispensable prerequisites to measurement.*

93 Standards

Quality Standards
Are International

*T*he International Organization for Standardization (ISO) is a worldwide federation of national standards bodies. Technical committees are formed in conjunction with international organizations, both governmental and nongovernmental, to prepare standards for topics of universal interest. *Quality management and quality systems elements* is a multipart document currently under preparation. *Part 1: Guidelines* has been completed; *Part 2: Guidelines for services* was in draft form in 1991.[5]

The role of measurement in service is a particularly vexing one. Early in the *Guidelines for services* draft, in the section titled "Characteristics of services," the authors note that "Many aesthetic or intangible characteristics subjectively evaluated by customers are candidates for objective measurement by the service organisation [*sic*]."

Undaunted by the challenge, the draft identifies areas that can (and should) be evaluated:

—facilities, capacity, number of personnel and quantity of stores;
—waiting time, delivery time and process times;
—hygiene, safety, reliability and security;
—responsiveness, accessibility, courtesy, comfort, aesthetics of environment, competence, dependability, accuracy, completeness, state of the art, credibility and communication.

The bulk of the 33-page draft is devoted to quality system principles and quality system operations elements. The operational elements are broken down into four processes: marketing process, design process, service delivery process, and service performance analysis and improvement. Ideas for organizing work, collecting data, and verifying results abound. A sample of the guidelines found in Section 5.2—Design Process—concerns the role of traditional statistical process control:

> 5.2.5 Quality control: Quality control should be designed as an integral part of the service processes to enable effective control to ensure that services consistently satisfy the service specification and the customer. Control should be effected by measurement and adjustment where necessary of the process characteristics to maintain the service characteristics within specified limits. Particular attention should be given to measurements at the interfaces between separate work phases.
>
> Design of service quality control involves three main steps. These are described below for the service delivery process but the principles apply for each service process.
>
> a) Identification of key activities in the process which have a significant influence on the specified service characteristics. (For example in a restaurant service a key activity to be identified would be the preparation of a meal and its effect on the timeliness of the meal being served to a customer).
> b) Analyse [*sic*] the key activities to select those characteristics to be measured and monitored in order to determine any necessary adjustment of the process. (Again using a catering restaurant example, a service delivery characteristic requiring measurement would be the time taken to prepare the ingredients for a meal).
> c) Defining actions, in response to the measurement of the key activities identified, to adjust the process so that each service characteristic is maintained within specified limits. (Continuing the catering restaurant example; effective deployment of staff and materials would ensure that the service characteristic of time taken to serve a meal would be maintained within the specified limits).

The concluding section of the draft version of the ISO standard for service quality recognizes that quality is a moving target:

> 5.4.4 Service quality improvement: There should be a programme [*sic*] for continuously improving the service quality and the effectiveness and efficiency of the complete service operation, including effort to identify:

—the characteristic which if improved would most benefit the customer and the service organisation [*sic*];

—any changing market needs that are likely to affect the grade of service to be provided;

—any deviations from the specified service quality due to lack of effective controls;

—opportunities for reducing cost while maintaining and improving the service quality provided, (this requires systematic methods for estimating the quantitative costs and benefits.)

The activities of service quality improvement should address the need for both short term and longer term improvement and include:

—identifying relevant data for collection.

—data analysis and giving priority to those activities having the greatest adverse impact on service quality.

—feedback of results of the analysis to operational management with recommendation for immediate service improvement.

—reporting periodically to senior management for a management review of long term quality improvement recommendations.

Personnel at all levels should be encouraged to contribute to a programme [*sic*] for quality improvement, with recognition. Members from different parts of the service organisation [*sic*] working together may be able to offer fruitful ideas that could be directed to improving quality and reducing costs.

Although not a final draft, the principles are identical to those found in writings by quality professionals from every country. While the language may change somewhat, the principles will not.

Axiom #**93** *Quality is an international concern with universally applicable solutions.*

Endnotes

Part One   On Leadership

1. Reprinted by permission of Fred Smith, founder, chairman, and CEO of Federal Express Corporation.
2. Copyright © 1989 by the American Society for Quality Control. Reprinted by permission.
3. Reprinted by permission of Chip Bell.

Part Two   On Participation

1. Reprinted by permission of Dr. David Levine and Dr. George Strauss.
2. Reprinted with special permission of King Features Syndicate, Inc.
3. Reprinted from March 1989 issue of *Psychology Today*, volume 23, pages 36 + .
4. Reprinted with the permission of Lexington Books, an imprint of Macmillan, Inc., from *Service Quality: Multidisciplinary and Multinational Perspectives*, by Stephen W. Brown, Evert Gummesson, Bo Edvardsson, and BengtOve Gustavsson, editors. Copyright © 1991 by Lexington Books.
5. Reprinted from January 28, 1991 issue of *Business Week*, by special permission, copyright © 1991 by McGraw-Hill, Inc.
6. Reprinted by permission of Noel Cunningham.

Part Three   On Measurement

1. Reprinted with permission of the *Worcester Telegram & Gazette*, copyright © 1990.
2. Reprinted by permission of Chief Ronald W. Miller.
3. Courtesy of Mutual of Omaha.
4. Calvin and Hobbes, copyright © 1990 Universal Press Syndicate. Reprinted with permission. All rights reserved.
5. Extracts of ISO 9004-2:1991 are reproduced with the permission of the International Organization for Standardization, ISO. The complete standard is available in the U.S. from the ISO member body, ANSI, 11 West 42nd Street, 13 Floor, New York, NY 10036, or from the ISO Central Secretariat, Case postale 56, CH-1211 Geneva, Switzerland.

Axioms for Action

On Leadership

Axiom #1: Leadership for quality must be active, obvious, and informed.

Axiom #2: When every employee is involved in improving quality, leaders emerge at every level. It becomes unnecessary to micromanage. The only preconditions are that employees know what is expected from them, know that the organization cares for them, possess the resources to do their jobs, and know they have authority to act.

Axiom #3: Management wisdom changes over the ages. Keeping abreast of current trends—including the trend toward quality improvement through a new relationship between management and nonmanagement—is one component of leadership. Management must face the challenge or concede the field.

Axiom #4: If after your reading and discussions on quality you are able to articulate your thinking more clearly, even in the absence of innovation, it may be thought of as new—or at least an improvement.

Axiom #5: Partial understanding of and involvement in quality can produce only partial success or total failure. Complete success requires a complete process. The only chance for a quality process to truly succeed is for a company to simultaneously attack all the issues: leadership, participation, and measurement.

Axiom #6: Until consensus is reached between executives and employees about how to go about achieving quality, there will be a great deal of wasted effort—or no effort at all.

Axiom #7: Americans are becoming more sensitive to quality in their role as consumers. Dr. Armand Feigenbaum has determined that in 1979 quality was given priority equal to price in only 30–40 percent of all buying decisions by consumers. By 1988, that figure had risen to 80–90 percent. To be consistent, Americans must also become more sensitive to quality in their role as business people. They can no longer resent being held accountable for the quality of their own goods and services.

Axiom #8: Familiarity with the writings of the quality gurus can furnish unexpected insights. Nuances are not always obvious on the first reading.

Axiom #9: Leadership techniques can be learned. While there is no question that some people are born natural leaders, the existence of great leaders is no excuse for the rest of us not to endeavor to become competent leaders ourselves. No one uses Einstein's genius in math as an excuse for not being able to balance the checkbook. Quality begins with leadership, and learning leadership begins with an appreciation of the options available.

Axiom #10: Policy statements and principles should be brief, clear, and believable. They are used as a touchstone for all employees to gauge whether or not actions are in conformance with the standards and values of the company's quality process. Milliken & Company, a 1989 recipient of the Malcolm Baldrige National Quality Award, focuses its employees on its quality policy by printing it on the back of all its business cards.

Axiom #11: Although the applications may vary in the military and business worlds, principles of military leadership are based on fundamental truths that make them appropriate in any situation in which one person is trying to lead another.

Axiom #12: Federal Express Corporation is right. It isn't enough for employees to have the answer to "What do you expect from me?" It is also necessary for employees to know "What's in it for me?" Companies that take care of their employees have employees that take care of their outside customers.

Axiom #13: **Humor**: 1. The quality of anything that is funny or appeals to the comic sense. 2. The ability to appreciate or express what is amusing, comic, etc. (*Funk & Wagnall*)

Good leaders have a sense of humor and know how and when to use it.

Axiom #14: Like it or not, every company has a corporate identity. It behooves a company to align its external image with its internal values. Often this can be accomplished through the use of symbols: Maytag and its lonely appliance repairman, Disneyland and its cheerful Mickey Mouse, the Peabody Hotel and its daily duck parades.

Axiom #15: A time constraint is the most common justification for the use of authoritarian leadership. In an emergency, most leaders instinctively take charge. The appropriate use of authoritarian leadership, however, is rarer than most people think—even when there is a pressing interest in getting things right the first time. Training helps individuals internalize participative and delegative skills. The rest is up to the individual.

Axiom #16: Attention to quality can increase a company's profits by lowering production costs, or by making it possible to charge higher prices, or both. There is no better long-term investment.

Axiom #17: If you understand the three leadership styles, you won't have any trouble with the textbook answer to this problem: The delegative approach is the most effective use of time and resources. Anyone willing to delegate when possible has time available for other tasks. There are, however, sometimes factors within an organization that make another choice appear desirable. Maybe the habits of the company make participative leadership the norm. Maybe those habits could be changed. There are always choices.

Axiom #18: This is a children's story, and it is possible to get the message after the first bird flies away. Or is it? The first part of the tale teaches one lesson: If you don't hear all the directions, it is impossible to do the job right. The last paragraph carries another lesson: If you don't listen until the end, you alienate others. Like the magpie, co-workers resent not getting a complete hearing. No matter how simple you think a message is, listen until the end.

Axiom #19: Love is what makes leadership work; it is what makes the difference between manipulating people and leading people. You cannot manipulate people into doing quality work.

Axiom #20: Intending to talk to "real people" is often not enough by itself. Outreach may call for a specific plan—with a detailed structure—to force executives to get out of the executive suite and interact with different layers of the company. This is especially true at the beginning of a quality process.

Axiom #21: Middle managers do have a unique problem with most quality processes. There is no getting around the fact that the role of middle managers will undergo a classic paradigm shift from being directors and micromanagers to being coaches and resources. This new model provides appealing opportunities for cooperation and innovation.

Axiom #22: Unless a company leadership team is prepared to back up its statements and slogans with quality performance, the money spent on halfhearted quality programs should be invested in enlarging the customer complaint department.

Axiom #23: The failure of past efforts can provide valuable clues as to a future course of action. In this case, programs to improve quality failed to establish a structure that enabled employees to actively participate on an ongoing basis. Learn your lessons from past experience and persevere—even in the absence of a supernatural phenomenon goading you to action.

Axiom #24: "Customers are easier to deal with than employees. You can hang up on customers." Once.

Axiom #25: Look beyond pervasive myths about quality. Many myths garner their popularity because they provide an excuse for inactivity. The reality is that there is no time like the present for beginning a quality process.

Axiom #26: The personal commitment of top management is absolutely essential to the success of a quality process.

Axiom #27: Be prepared for an initial outlay to cover quality-related expenditures. Time, materials, and expertise must be paid for. After start-up costs, however, a quality process will more than cover its own expenses. Quality professionals conservatively estimate that a well-run quality process yields a minimum of a 5-to-1 return on investment.

Axiom #28: The black box approach to leadership means delegating to subordinates without meddling in the details. It does not mean that a leader is off the hook; the leader is still responsible for what goes into the box and for the results that come out.

Axiom #29: Asking for help with a quality process can be a real shortcut, but don't let a consultant undermine your self-confidence. Rely on your own judgment if the advice seems inappropriate. Be sure the fit is right for you! It isn't enough to make the consultant look good.

Axiom #30: Simple can be profound. Sometimes a few words can get to the heart of the matter.

Axiom #31: Trust is conveyed to employees in everyday behavior. It is not enough to say you trust someone; you have to demonstrate it.

On Participation

Axiom #32: Participation presupposes that you are dealing with intelligent, cooperative, capable adults. If co-workers do not fit that description, participation presupposes that they can be encouraged to behave as if they do.

Axiom #33: If the corporate philosophy does not change one iota, if there is no structure or training provided, here is one time-saving and money-saving step that anyone can take: Ask your internal customers what they want. A degree of autonomy is available to everyone.

Axiom #34: On balance, the known advantages of participation outweigh the known disadvantages.

Axiom #35: Every human endeavor involving two or more people needs to be based on a common understanding of what rules apply.

Axiom #36: If a reason to celebrate arises, party. If it doesn't, look for a reason to celebrate.

Axiom #37: Wouldn't it be better to be a part of deciding what changes will be made rather than having to adjust to them?

Axiom #38: Communications are vital to a successful quality process.

Axiom #39: Service personnel are often the external customers' definition of quality. No matter what it says in the company service manuals, the customer only believes what he or she personally experiences. This puts an inordinate amount of pressure on the front-line employees of a service organization to be creative in meeting customer needs.

Axiom #40: If the quality movement in America ever gets organized to the point of choosing a theme song, it should be "Little Things Mean a Lot." It is the continual flow of small ideas that is the heart and soul of quality improvement. Being alert to every opportunity also makes it more likely that the big ideas will surface.

Axiom #41: Even a sound management practice can be reduced to the status of a fad if words are used without understanding. In the case of empowerment, everyone must not only be alert to possibilities for change, but they must also be able to make changes when appropriate. Only then will quality improve continuously.

Axiom #42: No system is inherently failure proof or failure prone. A lot depends on the company's follow-up procedures and how well they are executed. Dr. W. Edwards Deming states flatly that at least 85 percent of all quality problems can be laid at the door of management. In some companies, the percentage is higher.

Axiom #43: "Whistle while you work."—The Seven Dwarfs; Alternate Axiom #43: "Be happy at your work."—Mao Tse Tung

Axiom #44: When participation makes each individual's unique contribution work for the organization, it taps into one of America's strengths.

Axiom #45: Employees who feel capable of solving problems, do. This activity often takes place in spite of, not because of, corporate policies. Lack of initiative is often directly related to rules and regulations that limit alternatives or to inadequate training—both of which are beyond employee control.

Axiom #46: Employees are well aware when management abdicates responsibility. Allocation of resources, communications, training, teamwork/cooperation, and definition of specifications are all management issues. Unless management is willing to solve these problems, it cannot expect employees to solve problems in their own work areas.

Axiom #47: Continuous learning, returning to the classroom for formal instruction, as well as undergoing formalized mentor relationships, is needed to master the skills necessary to stay abreast of accelerating change. Companies that include quality-related subjects in their curriculum, in addition to traditional job skills, are better prepared to meet the future.

Axiom #48: Lower-ranking employees are the corporate memory. They know more about the production of products and services, and the processes that are used, than they (or anyone else in the organization) are aware of. Even when they are ignored, these men and women continue to do their best—and their best becomes so routine that they fail to realize how special their knowledge and their contributions are.

Axiom #49: The quality purists are valuable in that they force conscious thought to justify steps sometimes taken instinctively. Surprised at the axiom? Don't be. Part of improving quality is understanding why something works or fails to work. There will be lots of uncomfortable questions. Only when answers have been negotiated can you proceed with confidence.

Axiom #50: Teams begin with individuals. Respect for the different ways that different people process information is an excellent first step toward helping diverse personalities reach consensus.

Axiom #51: Be sure you are using the right perspective when you set your goal. Is the goal to inspect in quality, to tackle large problems, or to improve quality overall? Only 100 percent participation can achieve the latter.

Axiom #52: There is heavy debate in the field of quality over the relative merits of manufacturing versus service quality. Keep the differences in perspective. This is not an either/or situation. Why not include the best of both?

Axiom #53: When evaluating training materials, ask yourself what you would want to know as a team leader. Then design your course accordingly.

Axiom #54: Business depends on education. America's business leaders, such as David Kearns, former CEO of Xerox and now Under Secretary of Education, and John Akers, CEO of IBM, have made education a priority. Both come from companies that have seen the positive impact of well-orchestrated quality processes.

Axiom #55: Quality brings just deserts to all: customers, vendors, and providers.

Axiom #56: Recognition is an integral part of quality. People hear "thank you" in different ways. What pleases the giver may not please the receiver, and the receiver's opinion is what counts. Solve the problem by saying thank you three or more ways to each person—and let the recipient respond to what tickles his or her fancy.

Axiom #57: Formal team leader training is just the beginning. Team leaders deserve all the positive reinforcement they can get; after all, they are acquiring new skills for the company's benefit. On the practical side, such reinforcement can solidify lessons learned in the classroom.

Axiom #58: A *process* is quite different from a *program*. The first is designed to impact corporate culture—immediately and permanently. The second is an isolated event. Plan to be delighted with your *quality process* from the first—and to live with it happily ever after.

Axiom #59: The involvement and participation of every person on the payroll is necessary if a company is going to receive maximum benefit from a quality process. Exactly how that is achieved will vary, but in designing the company's quality process management must take into account all three types of quality opportunities: continuous, periodic, and episodic.

Axiom #60: The best combination is talent and teamwork. As a duo, its synergy is hard to beat—as GM will attest. After a sustained effort to build a culture of teamwork and customer awareness—and thanks to the investments and long-term commitment of top management—GM's Cadillac Division won the Malcolm Baldrige National Quality Award in 1990.

Axiom #61: Never underestimate the power of teamwork to improve quality. It can also be fun.

Axiom #62: Whatever approach a company chooses for a quality process, a common vocabulary will be necessary to communicate goals and methods effectively.

On Measurement

Axiom #63: One of the absolutes of quality is that you can't manage what you can't measure. Measurement tells you where you are and where you are going.

Axiom #64: Pareto Analysis (also called the 80-20 Rule) is a popular and useful measurement tool for identifying and prioritizing problems. This technique is readily accessible: Pareto Analysis need not be mysterious.

Axiom #65: A few well-chosen measures can alert a company to a problem that requires attention.

Axiom #66: Had it not been for the squeaky wheels in Japan, Tennant may not have been made aware of their eroding popularity in their biggest market until their customers began walking away. The opinion of customers must be aggressively sought out—even in the absence of complaints.

Axiom #67: Benchmarking—the process of measuring an organization's or an individual's current status and comparing it either to past performance or to the accomplishments of others—is a good common-sense first step to improving quality.

Axiom #68: Measurements are taken as a catalyst for change. Not all measurements, however, are taken with a set of calipers. Surveys are also a valid, and valuable, means of measurement.

Axiom #69: Quality and cooperation are inseparable in measurement, just as they are in leadership and participation. Beware the "Rumpelstiltskin Complex": quality control specialists who act as if their discipline is too arcane and complex for mere mortals. Quality control is most effective when it is designed into production processes for the use of employees at every level. Everyone can help with both the design and the implementation of quality control.

Axiom #70: Here is a case in clear violation of Dr. Joseph Juran's definition of quality, "Fitness for use." As an alternative, satisfying this three-part definition of quality would have prevented the problem:

- Quality in Fact—Meeting your own specifications.
- Quality in Perception—Meeting your customers' expectations.
- Customer—Anyone to whom you provide product, service, or information.

Axiom #71: When designing a program to increase customer satisfaction, a guarantee is just the beginning. A good design also includes plans to actively solicit customers' opinions.

Axiom #72: When you can document your solution with hard numbers, you are more likely to get what you want.

Axiom #73: Common sense isn't so common. Whenever there is an observable waste of time, money, and physical resources, there has to be a better way. True quality requires both effectiveness and efficiency. It may be easier to make excuses for the current state of affairs, but it won't solve the problem.

Axiom #74: It's far easier to say to outsiders, "Oh, yes, we believe that our employees are our greatest asset" than it is to say to employees, "You know what is right. Set your standards and do it." Trusting employees—believing that they are adults who want the company to succeed and then acting on that belief—is rarely better demonstrated than when dealing with questions of measurement. Given the opportunity and support, employees will set and maintain rigorous standards.

Axiom #75: Improvements can be achieved by putting the appropriate data in the right hands and then getting out of the way.

Axiom #76: While every employee makes decisions every day on whether or not tasks are being performed correctly ("Are we doing things right?"), management has the additional responsibility of deciding what tasks need to be performed

("Are we doing the right things?"). Value Analysis and Service Blueprints are two tools available to assist in this task.

Axiom #77: Abigail Van Buren puts it succinctly, "I say, always strive for perfection but allow for human error." George Fisher, president and CEO of Motorola, a 1988 Malcolm Baldrige National Quality Award winner, would agree, but he might add "but not too much of it." He talks about 6 sigma quality—a goal of only 3.4 errors per *million*. He hopes to be talking about errors per *billion* by 1992. That's pretty close to perfection.

Axiom #78: When wondering what to measure to improve quality, help is available. The *Application Guidelines for the Malcolm Baldrige National Quality Award* provide a universal and flexible tool for evaluating quality efforts.

Axiom #79: The individuals traditionally responsible for quality control are not made obsolete by a quality process. Their skills are an integral part of any quality effort. When quality control specialists share their skills with a wide range of employees, they become an invaluable asset to the company.

Axiom #80: While not offered as a guarantee, the legal tag in the first form is tantamount to a guarantee of nonservice. Implicitly, up-to-90 days is the *published measure* for what the company considers acceptable response time. It informs the reader that the customer cannot hold the publisher responsible for timely service. The company intended to protect itself in an unusual case; the result was to discourage the customer in virtually every case.

Axiom #81: A short course in logic is an excellent accompaniment to measurement.

Axiom #82: A Cost of Quality survey can educate employees as to the importance of prevention versus detection and correction. Survey results can also be a benchmark for progress and a source of ideas for improvement.

Axiom #83: There are occasions when precise measurements are necessary to assure a favorable outcome. There is no more reason to be concerned about taking these measurements on the job than there is in the home. Anyone who can follow a recipe, understand sports statistics, or read a map can use measurement on the job.

Axiom #84: Shifting the Cost of Quality into prevention isn't always easy, even when it pays off in dollars and cents. Preserving the status quo has its own appeal. For example, if a production facility begins making everything right the first time, what happens to the customer service department?

Axiom #85: Even public servants have customers. The same measurement tools used in the private sector to find out what the customer wants can be used in the public sector for the same purpose.

Axiom #86: When everyone in the company becomes a quality manager, everyone must be aware of the pitfalls of measurement. Mutual of Omaha has avoided the four reasons why quality managers fail, as given by Dr. Joseph Juran:

- Preoccupied with conformance to specifications rather than focusing on fitness for use.
- More concerned with appropriateness of their methods and procedures than with what is right for their business.
- Become in-grown, oblivious to the world around them . . . major concern is meeting the goals of the quality department with little regard for what is happening in other areas.
- Unfamiliar with, or cannot cope with, corporate culture.

Axiom #87: Measurements taken in the course of a quality process can be used to track progress. They can also be used to assign blame. In an organization that combines measurement with sound leadership and participation principles there is less potential for abuse.

Axiom #88: Just because a measurement can be taken doesn't mean it should be. Just because a calculation can be made doesn't mean that it must be made or that it makes sense.

Axiom #89: Variability is unavoidable. Using measurement tools aids employees in lessening its impact.

Axiom #90: According to Ron Zemke, "The true test of an organization's commitment to service quality isn't the stylishness of the pledge it makes in its marketing literature; it's in the way the company responds when things go wrong for the customer." The same is true with product quality.

Axiom #91: Measurements used incorrectly can be ludicrous. Even worse, taking irrelevant measurements is destructive to morale and can produce unforeseen negative results.

Axiom #92: With award-winning quality, leadership and participation are indispensable prerequisites to measurement.

Axiom #93: Quality is an international concern with universally applicable solutions.

Index

About the Authors

Patrick L. Townsend is a noted speaker and consultant on quality. From 1983 to 1987 he directed and coordinated the most active employee participation quality process in the country. In just three years, 250 quality teams at the Paul Revere Insurance Group implemented over 20,000 quality ideas, saving the company 16 million dollars and boosting its market position to number one. Mr. Townsend is the author of the best-selling book *Commit to Quality*, and he has written hundreds of articles. He is president of Townsend and Gebhardt—Advisers on Quality, a quality management and training company. Mr. Townsend lives and works in Holden, Massachusetts.

Joan E. Gebhardt collaborated with Patrick Townsend on *Commit to Quality* and is his partner at Townsend and Gebhardt. She honed her opinions on quality in a number of settings—she has taught in an elementary school, worked in a public relations firm, and sold electric motors; she has been an administrative assistant, a dorm mother, and a professional entertainer.